Praise for *Seeing Black and White in a Gray World* . . .

This little book is a must read for those who want a clean and clear account of the issues we face within United Methodism. John Wesley would have been delighted with both its style and content. We move beyond the sentimental preacher-talk and the pious middle ground; we come face to face with the benefits of straight-forward logic, accurate historical fact, and gracious engagement with the real alternatives before us. Both friends and foes need this brisk tonic if we are to make any progress in the debate that is raging all around us.

William J. Abraham
Outler Professor of Wesley Studies
Altshuler Distinguished Teaching Professor
Perkins School of Theology, Southern Methodist University
Dallas, Texas

As a pastor who leads a local church that is unashamedly God-centered and passionately people-focused, the issue of same-sex attraction is a regular part of our ministry. It seems to me sentimentality is ruling the day when it comes to this very tender, sensitive issue. Clear biblical teaching rooted in historical Christianity must trump a kind of mushy grace when it comes to the moral issues of our day for followers of Jesus. I believe Bill Arnold does that in this book.

Jorge Acevedo
Lead Pastor, Grace Church
A multi-site, United Methodist congregation
Cape Coral, Florida

Dr. Arnold makes a clear and convincing case supporting our current United Methodist stance on same-sex practices. He sets the issues within the context of classic, orthodox understandings of sin, salvation, and the nature and ministry of the church. His gracious and thoughtful presentation adds greatly to our ongoing conversation about human sexuality and God's Divine plan for our lives.

G. Lindsey Davis
Bishop, Kentucky Annual Conference
Louisville, Kentucky

It is no secret that United Methodists are deeply divided over the issue of homosexuality. Unfortunately, an even bigger threat to unity lies just beneath the surface—namely, the loss of intellectual virtue in debate. People on both sides of the issue routinely resort to caricature, intemperance, impatience, grandstanding, and logical fallacies galore. At our worst, we resemble a bad episode of *The Jerry Springer Show*. In stark contrast, *Seeing Black and White in a Gray World* is patient, courteous, respectful, and carefully reasoned. Indeed, Bill Arnold exemplifies a Wesleyan approach to argumentation. For this reason, even those who will likely disagree with his conclusions should read this book. And we should all seek to emulate it.

Jason E. Vickers
Associate Professor of Theology and Wesleyan Studies
United Theological Seminary
Dayton, Ohio

The United Methodist Church is covenantal in nature. For true connection and authentic community to exist, there must be clear agreements on issues of theology and practice. Dr. Arnold, reasoning through one of the most sensitive presenting issues straining our covenant, offers orthodox followers of Jesus solid Bible study, practical theology, and appropriate vocabulary to help negotiate the conversations facing us all in this season. I am grateful to Dr. Arnold, whose scholarship makes me a better pastor.

Carolyn Moore
Founding Pastor, Mosaic UMC
Augusta, Georgia

If you are looking for something that is well articulated, theologically rooted, fairly written, logically approached, and carefully documented then you will certainly appreciate this book! Dr. Arnold deals forthrightly and lovingly with the hard questions around our United Methodist struggle with same sex practices. He offers us a strong scholarly account of the history of the scriptures as well as an accurate accounting of our rich doctrinal heritage. This book is truly insightful and challenging as it moves us to the core issues in our debate on human sexuality. Wherever you find yourself in the debate, this is a must read!

Al Gwinn
Bishop, Retired, United Methodist Church

One of the most difficult conversations to have in the current ministry context is the conversation about same-sex practices. It is divisive in our denomination and challenging in our churches primarily because we err on the side of grace *or* truth. To be faithful witnesses of the Gospel, we must recapture what it means to be like Jesus, who was full of grace *and* truth. With this book, Bill Arnold leads both our heads and our hearts in that direction.

Bryan Collier
Lead Pastor, The Orchard UMC
Tupelo, Mississippi
Director, The Wesleyan Covenant Network

The issue of same-sex attraction is a challenging one for the church in our current cultural climate. Bill Arnold provides a way forward that is not only solidly reasoned and deeply rooted in Scripture and historic Christianity, but articulated with grace and sensitivity. *Seeing Black and White in a Gray World* is a positive contribution to a difficult conversation.

Kimberly D. Reisman
Executive Director, Next Step Evangelism Ministries
West Lafayette, Indiana

You can't build good practices on bad thinking. Presenting false dichotomies and then seeking some perceived middle way ironically stands as a stumbling block to understanding and resolving conflicts or tamping down ugly polemics. Bill Arnold's book shows how bad thinking—plausible though it seems—leads to more confusion and conflict rather than to healing and harmony. Arnold draws on the church's rich resources and illustrates by irenic yet pointed analysis that we must continue to search for true answers to difficult questions, especially with regard to thorny issues of sexuality. This is the kind of tool we need if ever we are to get serious about bridging denominational rifts.

Steve Rankin
Chaplain and Minister to the University
Southern Methodist University
Dallas, Texas

SEEING
BLACK&
WHITE
IN A GRAY WORLD

About the In All Things Charity Series

John Wesley is often credited with the saying, "In essentials unity. In nonessentials liberty. In all things charity."

As the world becomes more religiously pluralistic and societies and cultures grow more contentious and divided, it will behoove the church to gain clarity in its discernment of the distinction between essentials and nonessentials. We must not shrink back from boldly articulating the core truths of the Christian faith. At the same time, we must grow in the quality of our character as our very conversations witness to the gospel in the presence of a watching world. Said simply, our relationships within the church are the barometer of our witness to the world.

Jesus minced no words when he told his disciples that the authenticity of their association with him would be known only by the quality of their love for one another. Later in prayer, he would connect the loving unity of the church to the believability of the gospel. See John 17.

The apostle Paul, in the celebrated thirteenth chapter of his first letter to the Corinthian church, in essence tells us the absence of charity, or love, signals failure.

As a publisher, Seedbed does not want to avoid the difficult subjects of our time. Nor do we want to agitate the church with unnecessary controversy. For this reason, Seedbed created the In All Things Charity series. The series will contain books across a range of challenging issues. For the series, we are selecting authors who we believe embody the variety of character that enables them to demonstrate confidence in their point of view with truthful love in their approach.

SEEING
BLACK&
WHITE
IN A GRAY WORLD

THE NEED FOR THEOLOGICAL
REASONING IN THE CHURCH'S
DEBATE OVER SEXUALITY

BILL T. ARNOLD

seedbed

Printed in the United States of America

Paperback ISBN: 978-1-62824-099-3
Mobi ISBN: 978-1-62824-100-6
ePub ISBN: 978-1-62824-101-3
uPDF ISBN: 978-1-62824-102-0

Library of Congress Control Number: 2014932816

Cover design by Andrew Dragos
Page design by PerfecType, Nashville, Tennessee

SEEDBED PUBLISHING
Franklin, Tennessee
seedbed.com
Sowing for a Great Awakening

For the Kentucky Annual Conference,
and especially one of their senior leaders,
Rev. Walter L. Arnold

Other books by Bill T. Arnold

Encountering the Book of Genesis: A Study of Its Content and Issues
(Baker, 1998; paperback 2003)

Encountering the Old Testament: A Christian Survey
(with Bryan E. Beyer; Baker, 1999; second edition, 2008;
available in German, Chinese, Portuguese, Korean)

*The Face of Old Testament Studies: A Survey
of Contemporary Approaches*
(edited with David W. Baker; Baker, 1999; paperback 2004)

*Readings from the Ancient Near East: Primary Sources
for Old Testament Study*
(edited with Bryan E. Beyer; Baker, 2002)

1 and 2 Samuel: The NIV Application Commentary
(Zondervan, 2003)

A Guide to Biblical Hebrew Syntax
(with John H. Choi; Cambridge University Press, 2003)

Who Were the Babylonians?
(Society of Biblical Literature/Brill, 2004)

Dictionary of the Old Testament: Historical Books
(edited with H. G. M. Williamson; InterVarsity Press, 2005)

Genesis: The New Cambridge Bible Commentary
(Cambridge University Press, 2009)

Introduction to the Old Testament
(Cambridge University Press, 2014)

*Windows to the Ancient World of the Hebrew Bible: Essays in Honor
of Samuel Greengus*
(edited with Nancy L. Erickson and John H. Walton;
Eisenbrauns, 2014)

Ancient Israel's History: An Introduction to Issues and Sources
(edited with Richard S. Hess; Baker, 2014)

CONTENTS

PREFACE   xiii

CHAPTER 1: Seeing Gray That Isn't There   3
*Adam Hamilton's Attempt to See Gray in a World of
Black and White* ▪ *What Is a Fallacy and Why Does It
Matter?* ▪ *The Presenting Issue: Same-Sex Practices*

CHAPTER 2: Falwell or Spong? Really?!   31
Logical Mistake #1: The False Dilemma ▪ *The Issues
That Divide Us* ▪ *The Quest for the Middle Way*

CHAPTER 3: The Fork in the Road   63
Holiness or Hospitality ▪ *Reading the Bible
the Wesley Way* ▪ *Scripture Versus Experience?*

CONTENTS

CHAPTER 4: Promises and Pitfalls of Compromise   95
Scripture, Again ▪ *Humility or Boldness: Equal Virtues?*
▪ *Wesley's "Catholic Spirit"* ▪ *Compromise
or Compromise?*

CHAPTER 5: A Funny Thing Happened
on the Way to Utopia   129
Are You Liberal or Conservative? ▪ *The Image
of Utopia* ▪ *The Left-Handed Cyclist*

CHAPTER 6: Homosexuality at the Center   165
Myth #1: It's About Orientation ▪ *Myth #2: It's About
Liberation* ▪ *Myth #3: It's About Civil Rights*
▪ *So, What's It About?*

CHAPTER 7: Conclusions—Where Do We Go
from Here?   191

QUESTIONS FOR THE READER   199

PREFACE

This is a *very* different book than I typically write. Because this is different for me, I've decided to tell you about myself here in the preface. This seems to be the norm nowadays, as a way of informing you of my presuppositions, convictions, and values. Others involved in this debate have done something similar, and even though this is quite different from the way academics usually do things, here goes.

I am an academic in the field of biblical studies. I teach Hebrew and Old Testament studies in a theological seminary. Most of my teaching is focused on helping students become better readers of the Old Testament, especially in moving from the text of the Bible to sermon preparation. Over the years, my research has focused on interpreting the Old Testament (with commentaries on Genesis and 1–2 Samuel), as well as ancient Near

Eastern history. I've spent a good deal of time writing about Hebrew grammar and historical topics (such as the Babylonians in biblical times, and why they're important). I've also written an array of introductory materials for beginning students.

I am also an ordained elder in The United Methodist Church. I love our church. I love its rituals, its history and heritage, and I love its Wesleyan theology. Other than the influence of my godly parents, God worked through The United Methodist Church more than anything else to redeem my life, nurture my faith, teach me the Scriptures, confirm my calling, and ordain me to the ministry. I have also served as a delegate to two of our church's General Conferences.

My experience at General Conference in Tampa (April 24–May 4, 2012) gave rise to this book. On the way to Tampa, I decided to read something beyond my normal reading list, something considerably out of my narrow research interests. I needed something directly related to the denomination I was going to Tampa to serve. And so I chose Adam Hamilton's book *Seeing Gray in a World of Black and White*.[1] I chose Adam's book for several reasons, one of which is that I know and respect

---

1. Subtitled *Thoughts on Religion, Morality, and Politics* (Nashville, TN: Abingdon Press, 2008). I will occasionally also draw on his subsequent book, *When Christians Get It Wrong* (Nashville, TN: Abingdon Press, 2010).

the author. We have met a few times, and I have followed his ministry with interest. He has built a great ministry in our denomination, and continues to provide important and inspiring leadership in The United Methodist Church. Adam's several publications have provided the church with helpful resources for strengthening family life, deepening one's faith through forgiveness and reconciliation,[2] and he has provided leadership among the denomination's leading-edge pastors. In these ways and many others, Adam is a gift to our denomination.

I was also aware that Adam had taken a position quite different from mine relating to the UMC's Social Principle on human sexuality, and had become a leading voice to change our statements on this topic, as well as our requirements for ordination. Since Tampa 2012 was surely going to be another General Conference in which we would struggle with the issue, I wanted to understand Adam's approach.

I was not disappointed in Adam's honest and straightforward book seeking a "third way" through and beyond the controversies confronting the church today. I *was* disappointed, however, by other features of the book. I was surprised by the number of unsupported

---

2. With books such as *Making Love Last a Lifetime: Biblical Perspectives on Love, Marriage, and Sex* (Nashville, TN: Abingdon Press, 2004); *Forgiveness: Finding Peace Through Letting Go* (Nashville, TN: Abingdon Press, 2012); and others.

assumptions, errors of reasoning, and flawed arguments running throughout the book. I also had questions about some of the theological assumptions, and Adam's reliance on pragmatism, sometimes at the expense of theology. But I'm getting ahead of my story.

As much as I like and respect Adam Hamilton, I decided—against all my natural inclinations—to write this book in order to draw attention to various shortcomings in *Seeing Gray.* Is it possible that we in the UMC have not been discerning enough about Adam's teaching on the topic of same-sex practices? Perhaps his well-deserved status as a preeminent leader in our church has led us to be less than critical (by which I mean "analytical") about his position on this issue. I will show here that the reasoning used in his book is flawed on a number of levels, but especially in the tendency to make assertions as true statements that do not flow naturally from established premises. His approach, which I will use as representative of others arguing in similar ways, proposes a *simplistic alternative for a complex issue.* In *Seeing Gray*, Adam has set up a false dilemma between the Reverend Jerry Falwell and Bishop John Shelby Spong. From here, he moves to additional assertions and propositions that are either unfounded or illogical.

I want to repeat that I am only using Adam's book as representative of others in the same vein. *Seeing Gray* has been as influential as any, and merits a closer look. And I hope in this critique to showcase how such approaches offering middle-way solutions on the complex question of human sexuality are not, in the long haul, helpful to the church. The current UMC approach is already a balanced and healthy third-way alternative. We affirm the sacred worth of all people, and welcome everyone into the loving arms of our Redeemer. At the same time, we invite all to enter into the fullness of life with God through personal and social transformation into the image of Christ. This invitation extends to the highest ideals of human sexual expression, specifically a call to monogamous heterosexual love. This is indeed a third way between those who simply accept and celebrate same-sex practices on the one hand, and those who condemn both the practices and the people who experience same-sex attraction on the other. The UMC stands between these approaches, and offers a better way, a third way. But this third way is achieved through discerning and teaching the black-and-white truths of Christian faith rather than trying to find gray that isn't there. This may be said to be the centerpiece of my response and the core assertion of this book.

Chapter 1 ("Seeing Gray That Isn't There") explores Adam's arguments in an introductory way, critiques his general approach, and considers how his approach relates to the presenting issue of human sexuality. Chapter 2 ("Falwell or Spong? Really?!") considers a number of specifics in Adam's attempt to find a middle way between controversial issues. These first two chapters detail my critique of his book, and attempt to clear the deck in order to construct another way of thinking about these issues and of working through the debate over human sexuality in particular (chapters 3–6).

The rest of the book calls for a return to the rich theological resources and doctrinal heritage of our church. Chapter 3 ("The Fork in the Road") confronts the problems we encounter when we look for middle-way solutions that are not possible. Chapter 4 ("Promises and Pitfalls of Compromise") considers the dangers of seeking compromise as an end in and of itself, which may result in something no one wants—a surrendering of principles. Chapter 5 ("A Funny Thing Happened on the Way to Utopia") warns that change itself is not always a good thing, and that the church has a unique role in its relationship to culture. And chapter 6 ("Homosexuality at the Center") directly considers the most important social issue of our day, and turns to The United Methodist Church's theological resources for answers.

The church's debate in recent decades over human sexuality has been driven by deep emotion, and by experiences we have had with friends and family members who embrace and celebrate same-sex practices. Above all else, our debate has been buoyed by the prevailing winds of change in North American culture. Such foundations for the church's debate are inadequate and risky. In contrast, this book is a call for theological reasoning in the church's debate on this issue. I have chosen Adam Hamilton as my conversation partner. I hope you, as my reader, will remember that I have done so precisely because of my appreciation and respect for Adam. In recent correspondence with him, Adam has graciously reminded me that he and I agree on a great many centrally important points. I am quite certain he is right about that. The common ground we share theologically is vast, more so than the issues about which we disagree. In this sense, our disagreement on human sexuality is an in-house, family argument. It is my earnest prayer that the vast common ground on which he and I agree will be kept in view as you read through my critique of his work, and that this same vast common agreement will make it possible for the beautiful church we both serve to remain united in our mission "to make disciples of Jesus Christ for the transformation of the world."[3]

Because this topic is so important and so difficult to write about, I have consulted a number of friends and colleagues for their advice and input. The list of advisers

---

3. *The Book of Discipline of The United Methodist Church 2012* (Nashville, TN: The United Methodist Publishing House, 2012), 91, ¶120

is too long to include here, but you know who you are. Thank you. I am especially grateful to my sons David and Jeremy for numerous conversations on this topic. And to their brother, AJ, who would no doubt have joined these conversations had he not been fighting in Afghanistan at the time. Thanks to Rev. Aaron Mansfield, who helped with the "Questions for the Reader," and to Andy Miller and J. D. Walt of Seedbed for a number of helpful suggestions. My wife, Susan, has endured countless reports about this book for months, and made insightful comments on the final manuscript. I will always be grateful.

SEEING
BLACK&
WHITE
IN A GRAY WORLD

1

Seeing Gray
That Isn't There

Some things are perfectly obvious and true to anyone. Such truths require no further argument or persuasion. These are undisputed certainties. They are black or white.

This might include an assertion, for example, that the sky is above you as you read this book, or that the chair in which you sit is beneath you. One can think of exceptions depending on context. The astronaut in outer space may be thought of as having the sky around her, or the circus lion-trainer may hold a chair over his head. We understand these are exceptions. And besides, the word *sky* takes on a new meaning for the astronaut in space, just as a chair ceases to function as a simple chair when carried into a lion's cage, becoming a different thing altogether in the hands of a lion-trainer. These excep-tions do not change the simple black-and-white quality of the assertions that the sky is above you and the chair beneath you.

On the other hand, some topics are *not* perfectly obvious to all rational people. These are disputed assertions, about which sincere thinking people often disagree. Should Pete Rose be inducted into Major League Baseball's Hall of Fame? Should the US federal government be more involved or less involved in the affairs of its citizens? Would the Nazis have been victorious in World War II had Hitler not opened an eastern front against Russia? Most baseball fans, politicians, and historians have firm opinions on these questions, but most will also admit that these are not black-and-white issues but are instead "gray areas," or issues about which reasonable people can agree to disagree.

It gets more complicated, however. What counts as black and white may itself be up for debate. We humans get into intractable conflict with each other when we cannot agree over the shade of certainty or ambiguity an issue has. This is the background for the title of this book. The question before us is how to respond to a dispute in The United Methodist Church, in which opposing sides of the debate believe their positions are perfectly obvious and true. Each side considers its position a black-and-white certainty, an obvious truth. Yet the two positions are mutually exclusive. They cannot both be right.

The question I will address here is whether we need more gray in the world around us, or whether it would be better—when all is said and done—if we were to see more black and white.

Adam Hamilton's Attempt to See Gray in a World of Black and White

I take up this question because of a vigorous attempt by Rev. Adam Hamilton to encourage United Methodists to see more gray. Adam is a respected pastor in The United Methodist Church. He planted the Church of the Resurrection (Leawood, KS) in 1990 and has guided the congregation to become the largest UM church measured by weekly attendance. He is truly a remarkable leader.

When Adam published a book entitled *Seeing Gray in a World of Black and White*, he became a leading voice in the UMC's debate on a number of controversial issues.[1] We begin by summarizing his arguments because they

---

1. Adam Hamilton, *Seeing Gray in a World of Black and White: Thoughts on Religion, Morality, and Politics* (Nashville, TN: Abingdon Press, 2008).

have had widespread influence in the church. His arguments for seeing more gray reflect the views of many in the church today and will therefore serve us as a helpful representative in asking whether we might need instead to see more black and white.

Adam's call for finding gray is first defined as nothing less than establishing a new kind of Christianity, that of the *via media*, or "a Christianity of the middle way."[2] The stated purpose is to take a new approach to all controversial issues, listening carefully to both sides of our debate, and finding ways to integrate the legitimate aspects of both sides in order to forge a new way forward. Adam calls for a new reformation, drawing upon the best aspects of both fundamentalism and liberalism. He says this reformation will be led by people "who are able to see the gray in a world of black and white."[3] The goal of this reformation is to provide new understandings of the Bible to shed light on debates about creation versus evolution, the problem of suffering, abortion, homosexuality, war, faith, and politics. Quite an agenda!

Before we get too far along in considering Adam's call for a middle-road Christianity, I need to take up three of the central assumptions at work in his book.

---

2. Hamilton, *Seeing Gray*, xvi.
3. Ibid., xvii.

1. The Issues—We should note first that the various debated issues listed in the last paragraph, and discussed by Adam in *Seeing Gray*, are too diverse to be taken together. These include: the way we read the Bible (hermeneutics), science versus religion (in general), theistic evolution versus creationism (in particular), universalism versus particularism, the problem of suffering, abortion, homosexuality, war, politics, and a few others I haven't included here. All of these are issues Adam addresses in an attempt to find "a third way" between liberals and conservatives. (His use of the terms "liberal" and "conservative" is another problem, and I will devote a discussion to them in chapter 5.) This third-way approach is, for Adam, an attempt to constitute the "radical center" holding together the best of both extremes as part of a new Christian reformation.

Consider for a moment this long list of controversies. It might be misleading to suggest that this newly reformed Christianity can find a middle road through so many controversies, especially so many wildly diverse topics. I agree with Adam that these are some of the most important questions and debates of our generation. And I agree that a few of these have unfortunately moved the UMC to the brink of division. Moreover, I agree with Adam on his moderating positions on a number of these issues. One question we must deal with here is whether or not it is helpful, or

7

even possible, to treat them all together in one attempt to find middle ground.

For one thing, different groups will stand on different sides of some of these debates. Not everyone who agrees with Adam about theistic evolution will stand with him on the question of universalism. Someone's position on pacifism might put them in the "liberal" camp, while they also oppose all forms of abortion, making them appear quite "conservative." My point is that Adam's grouping of individuals into handy categories is simplistic and reductionistic, and makes it impossible to imagine finding a third way between liberals and conservatives. It is superficial to assume that all the debated issues in *Seeing Gray* can possibly have a third-way compromise that would move the church forward into a new future. These controversies are all too different from each other, and each has its own complex set of problems to address. For this reason and others, my response in this book will only touch on these briefly, while focusing especially on one of them, perhaps the most important and divisive one on the list.

2. The Objective—*Seeing Gray* presents an important but subtle shift away from truth-seeking as the primary objective in our debates. He argues that Christian participation in America's culture wars is hypocritical. Christianity has been used as a wedge in our culture wars because Christians have not taken seriously Jesus' warnings against straining gnats while swallowing camels (Matt. 23:23–24). He identifies "our quest for truth" with a separatist tendency that demonizes others and results in black-and-white thinking.[4] In one important passage of the book, Adam affirms the creeds of the church as important faith statements of early believers in their quest to identify the essentials of the faith. He also observes, however, that the creeds were "never comprehensive statements," as though any condensation of essentials could ever be comprehensive. In the next sentence, he states flatly, "Ultimately, what is needed is humility." He further asserts "humility is essential to Christian faith."[5]

Of course, we all agree that humility is an important feature of any orthodox formulation of the Christian faith. We learn first in the *ordo salutis* (Latin, "order of salvation") that we have sinned and are incapable of self-deliverance. We need a Savior. We need a loving Redeemer who is capable of doing for us what we cannot do for ourselves. Of course humility is intrinsic to Christian faith! But Adam's discussion of this topic is a distraction because it implies I am less than humble, even arrogant, if I do not agree on this topic or another. And it is surely questionable to say, "Ultimately, what is

---

4. Hamilton, *Seeing Gray*, 9–13.

5. Ibid., 14.

needed is humility." Is humility really what is needed in the church today? One could easily make the case that boldness and courage—also features intrinsic to apostolic Christianity—are needed today as much or more so than humility.[6] Indeed, boldness is not at odds with humility. The early Christians appear to have had both in abundance. Similarly today, when one is moved by conviction to speak out about this or that issue, it may require boldness and courage to do so. Whether one is prideful or humble in doing so is irrelevant to the validity of one's claims.

3. The Role of Pragmatism—Adam's book is firmly rooted in pragmatism. By this I mean decisions about controversial issues are often based on claims about what works or what is believed to be most effective in appealing to the greatest number of people.[7] At times, this pragmatism has a confirming role, coming along later to confirm what he has assumed to be true. So, for example, in his chapter on homosexuality, Adam explains how he came to his current position on the

---

6. It may also be less than humble to speak of the early church creeds dismissively, and then call for humility as essential to Christian faith.

7. Pragmatism may be defined as seeing truth as consisting, not in correspondence with facts, but in consistency with experience. This is similar to philosophical instrumentalism, which holds that the value of ideas is not in whether they are true but whether they are successful.

matter by sharing a sermon he preached to his congregation.[8] He grieved over the loss of "hundreds of people" in the year following the sermon, but he also "had more than a thousand people who joined the church during that same period of time."[9] The implication is clear. His new stance on same-sex practices reaches people; it works. The question needs to be raised: Is it legitimate to establish Christian practice along the lines of a business model in which measurable or numerical success determines truth?

Such pragmatism shows up more than once in *Seeing Gray.* But it rises to the surface most clearly in Adam's concluding chapter when he discusses the alarming decline of United Methodism since the 1960s. He acknowledges a host of reasons for the loss of membership. He then asserts that "conservative Christianity" (we'll come to problems with this language in chapter 5) is on the decline, and will continue to decline because it is becoming increasingly disconnected with emerging generations.[10] At the heart of his discussion is the notion that the church, and the UMC in particular, is losing this generation of young people. The twentysomething crowd is at risk

---

8. Hamilton, *Seeing Gray,* 165–87.

9. Ibid., 167–68.

10. Ibid., 227–28.

because we have not changed our stance on social issues, particularly on same-sex practices.

Adam assumes at critical junctures in the discussion of *Seeing Gray* that both United Methodism and conservative Christianity must get on board with the "Emerging Church" or risk losing this generation of young people. The Emerging Church is described as a growing movement of young believers signaling the beginning of a new era, and made up mostly of former conservatives. This is what Adam understands to be the "radical center" holding together the best of conservatives on the right and liberals on the left, and is the future of the church.[11] What I find surprising in this discussion is that there is no argument here for why anyone would *want* to be on board with the Emerging Church. The case hasn't been established that such a young persons' movement is retrieving the lost orthodoxy of the mainline church or advancing the gospel more faithfully than anyone else. Rather, they're growing, and we have to get with the growth program.

Is it true that this generation is lost to United Methodism because of our stance on human sexuality? Or is it just as likely or perhaps more likely that we would in fact lose more young people—and lose them faster—if we *did* change that position? It is possible that the evidence and arguments could be brought to the discussion that expose

---

11. Hamilton, *Seeing Gray*, 232.

Adam's assertion as unfounded, or at least challenge it as not established. One wonders if it isn't more likely that the largest and fastest-growing Christian universities and seminaries, campus ministries, and youth movements are ones that hold to traditional Christian definitions of morality and marriage. And perhaps the Emerging Church is just trendy, and what is needed instead is realignment with the early, primitive church.[12]

On the other hand, it could be that this whole point is irrelevant. My objection to Adam's pragmatism is that it misses the point. Whether he is right or wrong about the reasons for declining membership in the UMC, what does it matter? Should we settle controversial questions based on popular appeal (like a business demographic)? This is all too typical of American culture, in that we expect our church to settle disputes, or worse, to establish doctrine and practice, based on what the majority of our citizens believe to be true. What a new idea in the history of Christianity! In reality, it matters little what the majority opinion is among young people. Or among middle-aged people or older adults, for that matter. Christians should not settle moral issues on the basis of pragmatism.

---

12. Indeed, the insubstantial foundations of the Emerging Church movement are already crumbling under close scrutiny; Kenneth J. Collins, *Power, Politics, and the Fragmentation of Evangelicalism: From the Scopes Trial to the Obama Administration* (Downers Grove, IL: IVP Academic, 2012), 171–205.

13

And my objective here is to show that the approach to human sexuality argued by Adam Hamilton and others is simplistic, misleading, and hurtful to the church.

While we're in the neighborhood of relevance, we might further ask how such pragmatism plays out in global Christianity. Data collected for the century from 1910 to 2010 suggest a significant southward shift in Christianity's center of gravity.[13] In 1910, more than 80 percent of all Christians lived in the global North (Europe and North America). One hundred years later, in 2010, this had fallen to less than 40 percent, with a majority of Christians living in Africa, Asia, and Latin America. This trend seems likely to continue. The rising tide of Christianity in the global South is now outpacing its decline in the North, resulting in a net growth of Christianity globally. If we're being practical, we might ask whether the UMC's current crisis over human sexuality is relevant, seeing that the debate itself is limited to the global North. Again, from a strictly pragmatic perspective, what difference would it make what the dying portion of Christianity says about this issue?

Before moving on to specific logical problems in Adam Hamilton's quest for a middle-road Christianity, I

---

13. For these data and the assessment presented here, see Todd M. Johnson and Brian J. Grim, *The World's Religions in Figures: An Introduction to International Religious Demography* (West Sussex, UK/Maldon, MA: Wiley-Blackwell, 2013), esp. 7–131.

ask further whether this attempt to see gray in a world of black and white is really a new reformation of Christianity. Adam speaks of "holding together the evangelical and social gospels," of "combining a love of Scripture with a willingness to see both its humanity as well as its divinity," and finally, of "coupling a passionate desire to follow Jesus Christ with a reclamation of his heart toward those whom religious people have often rejected."[14] But these are features that characterized many of the *first* Reformers (especially the English Reformers, like John and Charles Wesley), and these are features of the church that have never disappeared entirely. What Adam is longing for here, it seems to me, is a revival or church renewal, not a reformation. Then the question becomes: Does church renewal come by finding a "middle road" through controversial issues, or by some other means?

What Is a Fallacy and Why Does It Matter?

So far I have pointed out some basic problems with three of the assumptions in Adam's book *Seeing Gray*. We have seen first that it is simplistic and reductionistic to argue that all the debated issues in his book can possibly have a third-way compromise that would move the church forward into a new future. These controversies are all

---

14. Hamilton, *Seeing Gray*, xvii.

too different from each other, and each has its own complex set of problems to address. Second, Adam believes an obsession with truth-seeking cannot be the primary objective of the church in today's culture wars. What the church needs is humility. And third, we have objected to the idea that these questions can and should be answered based on what works best. Such pragmatism is not legitimate footing for theological reflection. Adam appeals to the loss of membership in the UMC as a reason to change the Social Principles. But we have observed that there may be a multitude of other causes for membership decline, even if we grant that our Social Principles are one of those causes.

My next objective in this first chapter is to present as clearly as possible why I object to Adam's reasoning in *Seeing Gray*. In particular, I find problems with the logic underlying these three assumptions. In order to explain what I mean, I need to turn briefly to the once familiar (but now largely lost) world of logic, with its focus on presenting, understanding, and evaluating arguments.

An error in reasoning is called a "fallacy," and arguments based on erroneous arguments are said to be "fallacious."[15] We use the word *fallacy* in two ways. First,

---

15. Frances Howard-Snyder, Daniel Howard-Snyder, and Ryan Wasserman, *The Power of Logic,* 5th ed. (New York: McGraw-Hill, 2012), 34, 147–49.

we often use it in a general sense for anything we consider to be false or incorrect. But second, in a narrower sense, *fallacy* refers to a faulty or incorrect *process* of reasoning—a process that results in faulty or invalid conclusions. This is how I will use it here.[16] I intend to show how the processes of reasoning in Hamilton's book only *appear* to conform to the rules of sound argument but that they, in fact, do not conform to such sound reason. My aim is not simply to *assert* that something is false or untrue. I hope to show *how* and *why* the arguments for many of his assertions are inadequate or invalid.

There are many types of fallacies. The hardest to identify only appear coherent and consistent in the flow of the argument but contain an error somewhere along the way in the *content* of the argument itself. I'll point out the various types of fallacies as they become important in the discussion.

Now let us return to the three principal assumptions in *Seeing Gray*.

1. The Issues—Adam has combined a number of debated issues and called for a new reformation of Christianity providing a third way through all these difficulties. I have objected that each of these controversies

---

16. Of numerous resources available to help understand this topic, a still helpful introduction is W. Ward Fearnside and William B. Holther, *Fallacy: The Counterfeit of Argument* (Englewood Cliffs, NJ: Prentice-Hall, 1959). See their pages 3–4 for these two ways of using fallacy.

and debates has its own complex set of problems, and that it is superficial to argue that a third-way compromise is possible in each case. But why would I object to such a noble enterprise?

Adam's discussion combines numerous controversial issues, each one causing strife and contention in the church. One such debate pits young-earth creationists against those who accept evolution. Others are divided over same-sex practices. *Seeing Gray* assumes that because a compromise might be found in one case—a compromise that would bring healing and wholeness to the church, and move the cause of Christ forward—then such a compromise can and should be found in each of the other debated issues. The aim of his newly reformed Christianity would bring controversy to an end, ushering in a period of harmony among believers.

Of course, this sounds wonderful. But Adam's process of reasoning here is unacceptable (that is, fallacious) because he has assumed what is true of one controversial issue is true of the rest. His process of reasoning assumes an attribute of one item in the group to be true of all items of the group. This error in thinking is a fallacy involving *ambiguity*, a type containing a subtle confusion between two closely related concepts.[17]

---

17. Howard-Snyder, et al., *Power of Logic*, 166. There are four such fallacies of ambiguity (166–74). In the assumption that all

It does not follow that, because one or more of the controversial issues has a solution, therefore every controversial issue has a third-way solution available. Adam seems to assume that all controversial issues are the result of extreme positions on either end of the spectrum, in which case either (a) a solution is attainable through humility and dialogue, or (b) a solution is already present but not articulated properly. At times, however, the controversies are simple *either-or* options, in which no middle-way solution is possible. This merely illustrates that each controversy is unique and needs to be addressed individually.

On the question of evolution versus creationism, for example, I agree with Adam completely that a mediating position is possible and would be helpful for Christians. There is room for real compromise on so-called "theistic evolution," although we still have diverse ways of understanding precisely what we mean by God's use of an evolutionary process in creation. But it hardly follows to assert that similar solutions are possible with regard to our debates on human sexuality. Adam has grouped these controversies together and called for a third way between all the difficulties. This process of reasoning

---

controversial issues can be resolved by finding a third way, Adam appears to be closest to the fallacy of *composition* (171–72), involving "an invalid inference from attributes of members of a group to attributes of the group itself."

is not defensible. A helpful compromise in one case is no indication that such is possible in every case. And in fact, Adam admits that no such third-way solution is available on the question of same-sex practices. His chapter on homosexuality in *Seeing Gray* acknowledges how painful and divisive the issue is, presents a cursory survey of the biblical data (from a sermon he preached on the topic), and calls for an open and receptive ministry of local congregations (especially his church) to homosexuals.

I will return in chapter 3 to Adam's treatment of the biblical data. Here I simply point out that he has not, in fact, proposed a solution on this issue. This is no third-way or mediating position. In fact, in his call for local congregations to respond lovingly to homosexuals attending their services, I do not disagree.[18] But by falling into the ambiguity fallacy, Adam has assumed (a) that, as a compromise between creationism and evolution is possible, similar compromise is possible and should be sought on the issue of same-sex practices, and (b) that such a compromise, once found, would be helpful and healing for the church. Because Adam's process of reasoning here is faulty, his conclusion is not established.

18. And in some respects, this has been the position of the UMC for four decades. The intractable debate, of course, is over the acceptance and celebration of same-sex practices, and especially over ordination and same-sex unions as Christian marriage.

He may, in fact, be wrong on both counts. Such compromise on the question of same-sex practices may not be possible, and if it were, it could, in fact, be hurtful and harmful for the church.

2. The Objective—As we have seen, Adam criticizes some Christians for their quest for truth, certainty, and purity of doctrine, which he says often results in a tendency to separate from those who disagree and to demonize the positions of others. "Ultimately," he argues, "what is needed is humility."[19] I have objected that we all agree that humility is an essential feature of orthodox Christianity. Who would argue with his assertion that more humility is needed? The question here is whether this is really the missing characteristic of the church that prevents us from moving beyond our disagreements.

Adam's elevation of humility as our greatest need is an example of the *Red Herring Fallacy.*[20] Such reasoning often introduces an idea into a discussion that is irrelevant to the topic, and tends to divert attention from the original issue at hand. When he raises the need for humility in our dialogue as Christians, Adam essentially changes the subject. Are Christians today arrogant?

---

19. Hamilton, *Seeing Gray*, 13–14.

20. More technically the *Ignoratio Elenchi* Fallacy, in which premises of an argument are logically unrelated to the conclusion. The Red Herring Fallacy is a general fallacy of irrelevance; see Howard-Snyder, et al., *Power of Logic*, 159–60.

Sometimes. Does that mean they are wrong about social issues? Not necessarily. I agree that we need humility, but I do not accept Adam's logic that humility on all sides will lead to compromise that is healthy and helpful.

To follow this line of reasoning a bit further, it is possible the arrogant Christian may be correct in his or her convictions about traditional sexual morals. Another Christian may also be arrogant, while accepting the changing societal views of sexuality. Conversely, a humble Christian may be either for or against changing the church's position on same-sex practices. So you see, while humility is of course needed for all followers of Christ, it is not relevant to one's position on our debated issues. This is a red herring fallacy.

3. The Role of Pragmatism—The third concern I have raised in this chapter is Adam's pragmatism, or the impulse to settle difficult moral questions on the basis of what seems to work best. While Adam admits that many factors contribute to declining membership in the UMC, he believes the current unwillingness to change our position on same-sex practices is one of those reasons. I have countered that moral questions should not be decided on the basis of majority opinion.

That much is obvious. But what may not be so obvious are the logical fallacies at work in Adam's presentation. Indeed, there are at least three fallacies intertwined in Adam's pragmatic approach. Two of these logical errors are closely related, and all three are subtle and hardly distinguishable from each other. Only when we consider them separately can we see how mistaken it is to allow pragmatism to drive these important discussions in the church.

The first fallacy at the core of Adam's pragmatism is (a) *appeal to the people* (otherwise known as the "Ad Populum Fallacy").[21] This mistake in reasoning attempts to persuade by appealing to the desire to be accepted or valued by others. Part of the appeal of Adam's approach is that he says he offers a compromise that by implication will make the UMC capable of reversing our membership decline. A slight variation of this fallacy, also one of the seven so-called Fallacies of Irrelevance, is (b) *appeal to force* (or the Ad Baculum Fallacy), which attempts to defend one's conclusion with a threat to the well-being of those who need to accept it.[22] Such arguments need not be limited to threats of physical harm, like the Mafia's "offer you can't refuse." Appeals to force can also take the form of psychological well-being, and in this case, institutional well-being. Is the future of the UMC in jeopardy? Is our beloved church on the verge of

---

21. Howard-Snyder, et al., *Power of Logic*, 155–56.

22. Ibid., 153–55, and for the seven Fallacies of Irrelevance, see 149–60.

schism, cultural irrelevance, or possible extinction? Well, yes. Does the church need to change its position on same-sex practices, or else face continued decline? It hasn't been established, in my view, that the UMC decline is a result of our stance on same-sex practices, either singly or together with other causes. Such appeals to "the people" or "to force" are simply wrong-headed.

A third and even more subtle logical error in Adam's pragmatic approach is the (c) *False Cause Fallacy*.[23] In such reasoning, one *possible* cause of something is assumed to be a (or *the*) cause although other unstated causes may, in fact, be at work. The most common form of this logical mistake is sometimes called *post hoc, ergo propter hoc*, "after this, therefore because of this." This occurs when someone assumes that because event X occurred before event Y, then therefore X must have caused Y to happen. This form of false-cause reasoning is precisely at work in our current debates whenever someone implies that the 1972 decision to add a statement to the Social Principles naming same-sex practices as "incompatible with Christian teaching" led

---

23. Howard-Snyder, et al., *Power of Logic*, 183–86. Appeals to "the people" and "to force" are Fallacies of Irrelevance, while the False Cause Fallacy belongs to a group known as Fallacies of Unwarranted Assumptions, 177–88.

to the church's decline ever since. The cause-and-effect connection between that statement in 1972 and the UMC decline in membership is far from a certainty. The argument carries no force.

I agree wholeheartedly with Adam Hamilton that we need a renewal or revival in the UMC. (Notice that I am not calling for a new reformation of Christianity.) But this is not the same thing as expecting to find resolution to all these debates. Perhaps the renewal we long for is delayed for other reasons. Some would suggest (and this argument would have as much logical explanatory power as the arguments Adam has put forward) renewal is delayed *because* we are having such debates! Perhaps a study of renewal movements in the history of Christianity would find such movements marked by an impulse to return to primitive, early church emphases, rather than innovations in cultural understandings or compromises on social issues. But this is getting ahead of our story.

For now we have observed that Adam's basic assumptions (compromise is possible on all controversial issues, humility is needed over truth-seeking, and pragmatism as a guiding principle) are marked by fatal flaws of reasoning. Before moving forward now to address details beyond these three basic assumptions, I need to explain why my response will be focused especially on one of the controversial issues presented in *Seeing Gray in a World of Black and White.*

The Presenting Issue: Same-Sex Practices

This book addresses the question of human sexuality, and especially same-sex practices, as the "presenting issue" in our current debates. A *presenting issue* is an initial or first-level question that needs resolution. Often, such pressing questions expose other *underlying issues* that are really at the heart of the struggle. In this book, I take up the debate over same-sex practices as the presenting issue in the UMC, while acknowledging that a number of underlying issues are just as important. These include, above all else, the way we understand divine revelation and the nature of Scripture, the operation and results of God's grace in our lives and in the world, and our understanding of our denomination as a global church. Human sexuality is the presenting issue, but it requires us to address a number of underlying issues as well.

By writing this book, I'm trying to be honest about this presenting issue as the one that threatens to splinter our church. I recognize that this will expose me to the accusation that I am a one-issue, narrowly focused member of the church by addressing this issue directly. In order to anticipate that objection, I reveal a bit more of myself here.

I come to the task of writing this book and addressing this issue reluctantly. This topic, even this style of writing, is not my most natural comfort zone. I would frankly rather be doing other things. I reject the accusation that I am too narrowly focused here by simply reminding you as my reader that human sexuality, and specifically, what we as United Methodists say about homosexuality, has become the presenting issue for more than forty years. The convergence of issues threatening to divide our church today are deep-seated and essentially theological in their foundations. We differ on our understanding of Scripture, as we will see, and everything that flows from it in our theological task. At the General Conference in Tampa (2012), I sadly concluded that even our understanding of our church's wonderful mission statement is dramatically different: "to make disciples of Jesus Christ for the transformation of the world."[24] We cannot seem to agree on what it means to make disciples, and we have different views of transformation.

As Bishop Timothy W. Whitaker once observed, the problem we have when we talk about this presenting issue is that "the language being used is laden with assumptions on which there is no agreement."[25] With

---

24. *The Book of Discipline of The United Methodist Church 2012* (Nashville, TN: The United Methodist Publishing House, 2012), 91, ¶120.

25. Timothy W. Whitaker, "The Church and Homosexuality," http://www.flumc2.org/pages/detail/967, accessed May 31, 2013.

Bishop Whitaker, I prefer the phrases "same-sex attraction" and "same-sex practices" and will use these almost exclusively throughout. These phrases are neutral in the sense that they do not take up the possible causes of such attraction and practices. In this way, we can have the debate without advocating for such practices, which is implied in words like "gay" and "lesbian," or endorsing one's existential self-identity, implied by "orientation." Similarly, "homosexuality" has its own negative connotations, and is a relatively recent word in human discourse. Bishop Whitaker recasts the debate, and explains further the importance of our words.

> [T]he church views our identity in terms of our relationship to God, not in terms of our sexual identity. Once the church succumbs to the idea that our basic identity is sexual rather than theological in nature, then the church has already lost its way in the discussion. This is not to say that our sexual being is unimportant, but it is to say that it is more appropriate for the church to first view people as persons who are created in the image of God before it says anything about their sexual identity.[26]

Regardless of what one believes to be true about this issue, we can all celebrate our church's affirmation that

---

26. Whitaker, "The Church and Homosexuality,"

SEEING GRAY THAT ISN'T THERE

"all persons are individuals of sacred worth, created in the image of God" and that "God's grace is available to all."[27] In what follows, I commit to speaking to and about my sisters and brothers who disagree with me on this question in a way that is honorable and sensitive. I will make every effort to refrain from using hurtful and derogatory language. Our UMC statement identifies as incompatible with Christian teaching "the practice of homosexuality," *not* those individuals who experience same-sex attraction. I desire always and everywhere to respect my brothers and sisters who disagree with me on this issue. I know my own need for God's grace and mercy, and trust that you my reader will be equally gracious and sensitive to me.

In conclusion, Adam Hamilton's call for a new Christian reformation, resulting in a church that sees more gray than black and white is wrongly argued from the start. The case has not been established that this is what the world today needs. Perhaps what the world needs is a church willing to seek more black and white than gray.

---

27. *2012 Book of Discipline,* 111, ¶161F.

CHAPTER

2

Falwell or Spong?
Really?!

A dam Hamilton begins his book with an anecdote.
It was 1991. He was watching television while
preparing for work, and saw an interview with Rev. Jerry
Falwell, pastor of Thomas Road Baptist Church, together
with Bishop John Shelby Spong, Episcopal bishop of
Newark, New Jersey. Falwell at the time was the most
visible fundamentalist Christian on the scene, and Spong
the most visible liberal Christian. Adam found himself
in sympathy at times with Spong but at other times with
Falwell. He felt torn. In frustration he objected, "These
two cannot be our only options for being Christian!"[1]

_____

1. Adam Hamilton, *Seeing Gray in a World of Black and White:
Thoughts on Religion, Morality, and Politics* (Nashville, TN: Abingdon
Press, 2008), xiii–xvii.

Reverend Falwell eventually fell into extreme positions, often shared by fellow fundamentalists, like Pat Robertson, such as blaming everything wrong with America on the ACLU, abortionists, and advocates for homosexuals. At the other extreme, Bishop Spong discarded historic doctrines of Christianity.

Adam acknowledges that Falwell and Spong represent the "extremes of the last quarter century," and then calls for a middle way between them. This he believes would be a "centered or balanced faith," a Christianity of the "middle way." Adam asserts that any controversial issue about which intelligent Christians disagree "likely has important truth on each side of the debate." He asserts further, without any justification for this statement, that "the key is to listen to both sides and look for ways to integrate the legitimate concerns of each side, often forging a new way forward, or at least plowing forward while taking seriously the views of the other."

Of course, who would disagree? This is a simple principle of civil discourse: whenever we find ourselves in disagreement with others, we should learn to hear and take their views seriously. This is something we all learn, or were supposed to have learned, on the playground in elementary school. I in no way disagree with this assertion.

But Adam goes further by claiming that finding third-way compromises to our disagreements would generate a "new reformation" for Christianity. He is bold enough to claim that "Christianity's next reformation will strike a middle path between Jerry Falwell and John Shelby Spong." And furthermore, that "this reformation will be led by people who are able to see the gray in a world of black and white." Who are these gray-seeing new reformers? Presumably Adam's proposals will lead the way in this new reformation.

I hinted in the previous chapter that proposing anything like a new reformation of Christianity is overreaching. In fact, it might be argued that the *first* Reformers (Luther, Calvin, and others) accomplished the Reformation by not making compromises at all! The history of Christianity would suggest that *their* Reformation was the result of insisting on black and white rather than finding gray. One wonders whether a Reformation of Christianity would have occurred at all had Martin Luther made compromises with the Roman Catholic Church.

But despite the overstatement, let us take up and consider Adam's proposition that a renewal of Christianity will strike a middle path between Falwell and Spong. Such a renewed Christianity would draw together the best of fundamentalism and liberalism into a gospel that holds together the evangelical and social gospels, would consider both the divine and human dimensions of Scripture, and would reflect both a deep personal faith in Jesus and a heart for social justice.[2] How, might you ask, could I possibly disagree with so noble a goal?

I begin by asking: What's wrong with this picture? Falwell or Spong? *Really?!*

Logical Mistake #1: The False Dilemma

So, what's wrong with this picture? Well, for one thing, it's just not true. Falwell and Spong are not our only choices, and never have been. Christians have numerous alternatives on each of the debates before us. None of us is obligated to identify with either Falwell or Spong. From the very beginning of his book *Seeing Gray*, Adam Hamilton sets up what is known as a "false dilemma" as part of his argument for a middle-road Christianity.

The *Fallacy of False Dilemma* is one of five logical errors involving unwarranted assumptions.[3] These are arguments based on assumptions that stand in need of support or have not been otherwise established. Such arguments carry no force. Specifically, the false-dilemma error asserts an unwarranted assumption that reduces the number of alternatives to be considered.

---

2. Hamilton, *Seeing Gray*, xvii.

3. Frances Howard-Snyder, Daniel Howard-Snyder, and Ryan Wasserman, *The Power of Logic*, 5th ed. (New York: McGraw-Hill, 2012), 177–88, and specifically for the Fallacy of False Dilemma, see 180–81.

Most of these arguments assume, without justification, that there are only two possibilities to think about, when in reality there are three or more to consider. They fail to recognize middle options excluded in the argument. Here is an example:

> I'm tired of all these young people criticizing their own country. What I say is this, "America—love it or leave it!" And since these people obviously don't want to leave the country, they should love it instead of criticizing it.[4]

The unwarranted assumption is that there are only two possibilities. One must love America uncritically or pack up and move elsewhere. But surely one could respect America, live in it, and obey its laws without *loving* the country (whatever one might mean by "loving" America). Conversely, it would seem possible to love America (again, whatever that might mean) and live within its borders without accepting every aspect of its society uncritically. The speaker is simply setting up a false dilemma by assuming these are the only two options.

So back to my question: Falwell or Spong? *Really?!* Adam has used the false-dilemma fallacy when he sets up the Falwell-Spong contrast at the beginning of

---

4. Ibid., 180.

his argument.[5] His book is thus based on the premise that Christians are hungry for a middle way between the extremes. He offers to guide the reader through the debates of the church today that threaten to divide Christians, taking the best of fundamentalism and the best of liberalism, and combining them. This will, he believes, offer a newly reformed Christianity that is centered and balanced, and which, he implies, holds correct convictions on these debated issues.

But we Christians—especially we Methodists—are not so limited. There are many alternatives between Falwell and Spong, options considerably less extreme than either of them. And these options do not necessarily constitute a third way between them, nor are they a combination of the best features of both extremes. There are many arguments to the right on the theological spectrum that are much less extreme than Falwell. Similarly, there are numerous views to the left that are less extreme than Spong. None of these others necessarily constitute a compromise to either position, or a "third way." The need to find a third way is exaggerated by identifying

---

5. Technically, Adam *claims* to identify a dilemma, which he then asserts is false, before offering a way beyond the stalemate. I deny that the dilemma exists at all, asserting instead that we have very many other options on all the issues before us. Either way, the dichotomy between Falwell and Spong is a contrived way to set up the argument.

these as the only options. Adam's quest for a third way in every debate is misguided by the false perception of only two options, and these extreme ones. He has over-stated the dilemma.

Adam is correct that these are not our only options for being Christian. In fact, he has already identified these two—Falwell and Spong—as extremists, a funda-mentalist and a heretic.[6] Adam then complains that "when the people representing the Christian community are Jerry Falwell or Pat Robertson on the one side, and John Shelby Spong on the other, you end up with a wide gulf in between with no one articulating a middle way." His book *Seeing Gray* is then offered as an attempt to find the "middle way" reforming Christianity. By mustering up enough humility and listening carefully to both sides of every issue, we are offered compromises on the debates that threaten the church.

Of course I agree with Adam that our culture is not listening to balanced voices that articulate the Christian faith (especially the media). Traditional Christian answers are not sensational enough to capture the

---

6. To be fair, Adam doesn't use the term "heretic" to describe Bishop Spong. But he observes that Spong "discards nearly all of the historic doctrines of the Christian faith," which is characteristic of heresy. Since Bishop Spong has essentially rejected traditional theism and Christology, the term "heretic" may not be out of the question.

imagination of today's news media. We sound jaded and old-fashioned in today's society. Perhaps that's unavoidable. At the same time, it needs to be said that we have never been limited to Falwell and Spong. Christianity and its answers to life's biggest questions have never been reduced to the extreme positions on either side of the theological spectrum.

The question is whether compromises along the middle path between these two extremes really bring us to Christianity, reformed or otherwise. Does a middle-road Christianity provide the answers? The truth is, there are and always have been many other options available for understanding the truths of Christianity, and most of them aren't new. This chapter will briefly consider most of the controverted issues in Adam's book, and conclude that traditional Methodism has always offered a balanced and "centered" option for Christians. We don't need a newly reformed Christianity. We need instead a Methodism that is renewed and empowered to continue the social work of spreading scriptural holiness across the land, as the early Methodists did.

The Issues That Divide Us

Here I take up the topics Adam Hamilton discusses in *Seeing Gray* to test the claim that what he offers is a middle way forward for Christianity. These will be brief, because my point is not to rehearse all the facts and arguments in each case (and two will be taken up in more detail later). But this exercise is merely to test the theory: Is it legitimate to find a third way between these two extremes, Falwell and Spong?

1. Scripture

The false dilemma is nowhere more evident than in Adam's discussion of the Bible. He first discusses fundamentalists who embrace "inerrancy" and who insist on a literal reading of Scripture. He cites the official statement of faith of the Evangelical Theological Society as typical of this group, and sums up by saying that the "most conservative" in this camp affirm "a creation that occurred in the last ten thousand years," and some also reject "the idea of women serving in leadership in the church."[7]

The alternative, in Adam's presentation, is illustrated by the famous Jesus Seminar. Beginning in the 1980s, the Jesus Seminar was composed of fewer than a hundred scholars who used variously colored marbles in voting to determine their collective views on the historical Jesus of Nazareth. They concluded that only about 18 percent of the sayings of Jesus in the Synoptic Gospels go back to Jesus himself, or represent something he said. Only

---

7. For quotes in this paragraph see Hamilton, *Seeing Gray*, 59–71.

one saying in the Gospel of John has anything to do with the historical Jesus (John 4:44). Essentially, according to many of the scholars of the Jesus Seminar, Jesus can be identified as a man born naturally to human parents, who did not perform miracles, and whose death has nothing to do with forgiveness for sinners. Many also denied the bodily resurrection of Jesus.[8]

Adam complains that liberals err on the side of overemphasizing the Bible's humanity at the expense of its divine origins. Conservatives, on the other hand, overemphasize the Bible's divinity at the expense of its human origins. (I will return in chapter 5 to the inadequate concepts "liberal" and "conservative.") As a result, Adam concludes that "the truth and place of balance seems to be somewhere in the gray between these two."[9] He argues for a middle way between these extremes, which takes seriously both the human dimensions of the Bible (the individual human authors, with their distinctive vocabulary, style, theology, and culture) and the divine dimensions of the Bible.

---

8. Thomas H. Olbricht, "Biblical Interpretation in North America in the 20th Century," in *Historical Handbook of Major Biblical Interpreters*, ed. D. K. McKim (Downers Grove, IL: InterVarsity Press, 1998), 541–57, esp. 554–55; Dale C. Allison Jr., "Jesus Christ," *NIDB* 3:261–93, esp. 263–64.

9. Hamilton, *Seeing Gray*, 66.

His analogy for such an approach is the Eucharist, or Holy Communion. As the ordinary bread and juice (or wine) become instruments of God's grace in the act of Communion, so the Bible is the means of God's grace in our minds, lives, and actions. The Bible is a kind of Eucharist, he concludes, and he offers this as a middle way between the extremes.

With the ghosts of Falwell and Spong haunting our imaginations, Adam would have us believe we are trapped between these two: fundamentalist inerrantists on the one hand, and historical minimalists on the other. But this dilemma will never do. It simply isn't true and never has been.

I will return in the next chapter to this question of the role of Scripture in the lives of Christians. But for now, it is enough to say that Adam's quest for a third way between inerrantists and skeptics is misguided and unnecessary. His proposal is *misguided* because it's a false dilemma; these have never been the only two options. Christians have always and everywhere had many other options for understanding the role of the Bible. His proposal is *unnecessary* because we have it! Look no further for a balanced and healthy view of Scripture. The United Methodist Church offers it. In fact, it's deeply rooted in our wonderful Wesleyan heritage, now more than two hundred years old.

In reality, our Methodist understanding of Scripture, at least when it is thoroughly Wesleyan, has never been tempted by either of these two extremes. We clearly understand the Bible as the instrument through which "the living Christ meets us in the experience of redeeming grace."[10] In other words, we Methodists see Scripture as a means of grace, somewhat like the Eucharist. It is the primary way God pours his grace into our minds and lives. On the other hand, we also understand the Bible as "the words of human beings inspired by the Holy Spirit," so that we are committed to reading it "within the believing community," in proper context, and "aided by scholarly inquiry." The theological task of United Methodism aims to "draw upon the careful historical, literary, and textual studies of recent years."

Look no further for a balanced view of Scripture. United Methodism's position is neither fundamentalist nor minimalist, and never has been. We have long since represented a healthy understanding, valuing both the human and divine dimensions of Scripture. Methodism accepts the Bible as a means of grace (somewhat like the Eucharist), while also leading the way in scholarly investigation of the human side of the Bible. Neither the Evangelical Theological Society nor the Jesus Seminar is a natural association for Methodists.

------

10. *The Book of Discipline of The United Methodist Church 2012* (Nashville, TN: The United Methodist Publishing House, 2012), 81, ¶105, and other quotes in this paragraph.

Adam's critique of inerrancy, with which I completely agree, is really a misplaced criticism of Reformed (that is, Calvinistic) strands of American evangelicalism. But the answer is not some new compromise with fundamentalists. I don't think we want to take the best of that approach, and somehow fold it into a new Christianity. And what is the best of fundamentalism? Instead, the answer is already in our hands in the form of our Wesleyan way of reading Scripture.

I also agree with Adam that the historical minimalism of Spong is to be rejected. And again, the answer is not some sort of compromise with such skepticism. What is the best of skepticism? In reality, our wonderful tradition in The United Methodist Church is already a different way forward. The dilemma between Falwell and Spong doesn't exist for us, and no compromises are needed to find balance in the way we read Scripture.

On this first and perhaps most important controversial issue—that of the Bible—I find that Adam's false dilemma is misguided and unnecessary. We Methodists have, in our best moments, always been less identified with either fundamentalists or minimalists than we have been identified with our founder, Mr. Wesley himself.[11] Furthermore, it is misleading to suggest that finding "balance" in the way we read the Bible will result

---

11. See the next chapter for more on this important topic.

somehow in "seeing gray." Is it equally possible that a balanced way to read the Scripture will result in more black and white than gray?

2. Science

Next, Adam takes up the seventeenth-century conflict between the Roman Catholic Church and Galileo as representative of the way Christianity and science relate to each other.[12] Of course, the church was proven wrong about the sun revolving around the earth, and Galileo's heliocentrism was proven right. Religion insisted the earth was the center of the universe, and science corrected that view.

I agree with Adam that a balanced view of the relationship between science and religion accepts them both as "partners in a quest for knowledge."[13] Much of the perceived conflict today between science and religion is just unnecessary and wrong. We need to correct the idea, often assumed by many Christians today, that there is an inherent and unavoidable conflict between science and Christianity.

Adam describes the church's dispute with Galileo as a conflict between "a scientific theory" and a "literal

12. Hamilton, *Seeing Gray*, 73–78.
13. Ibid., 75.

reading of Scripture."[14] However, there was a great deal more involved. Science, as such, was only beginning to emerge in the seventeenth century as an alternative understanding of the universe. There was no established scientific community with a wide consensus on the nature of the universe. Those in the church who raised questions were not blindly refuting established scientific theories, but assessing the validity of the entire scientific enterprise. And the Roman Catholic Church was not simply entrenched in a literal reading of Scripture. There were larger social and cultural issues involved in the debate as well.

In fact, the single episode of Galileo cannot be used to typify the relation of science and religion.[15] From the beginning, Judaism and Christianity led the way in desacralizing and depersonalizing the natural world in a way that made science possible centuries later. The condemnation of Galileo was out of character for Christianity, and in some ways was only the result of the Roman Catholic Church's entrenchment in the great conflict of Reformation and Counter-Reformation. The rejection of

---

14. Hamilton, *Seeing Gray*, 74.

15. For more on what follows in this paragraph, see Stephen M. Barr, *Modern Physics and Ancient Faith* (Notre Dame, IN: University of Notre Dame Press, 2003), 4–18. Barr shows that there has never been a conflict between religion and science, but only between religion and materialism.

Galileo was, in fact, an anomaly—a blip on the screen, if you will—because the church had overwhelmingly been friendly to scientific inquiry and supportive of its findings. Many of the great founders of modern science were deeply religious thinkers, including Copernicus, Galileo, Kepler, Newton, Ampère, and others.

The "Galileo Affair" may be taken as a helpful lesson in the way Christians learn from the latest scientific investigations. But does it serve us well as an example of conflict between polarized positions, between which Christians found a compromise? On the last page of this chapter, Adam asserts, "Between the black-and-whiteness of the conflict between science and religion is a place where both are valued for what they offer us as human beings: a place where we don't have to choose between science and religion."[16] Well, yes, Christians have understood for centuries that faith can learn a lot from science. But Adam goes further. "They [science and religion] are not adversaries, but two different ways of helping us understand the universe and our place in it. Those who recognize this have come to appreciate the value of gray."[17]

The implication is simple. If one agrees with Adam that Galileo was right and the church was wrong, and

---

16. Hamilton, *Seeing Gray*, 78.
17. Ibid.

that the perceived conflict between science and religion is unnecessary, then we will also learn to see "the value of gray." Presumably, as we learn to see more gray, we will also agree with Adam on other controversial issues as well.

There's just one problem. The conflict between the church and Galileo was not resolved by compromise, or by finding a third-way solution. Galileo was either right or wrong. In this case, there simply was no gray! Galileo was proven right because he defended the black-and-whiteness of his convictions, against gray. No compromise was found, because none was possible. The only real conclusion to be drawn in this case is that we must remain open to scientific investigation, not that we need to learn to value gray over black and white. Sometimes in a genuine dilemma, black and white is preferable to gray.

3. Human origins

Related to the question of science, Adam next takes up the controversy on evolution and three possible Christian responses to it: young-earth creationism, intelligent design, and theistic evolution.[18] I agree with Adam that theistic evolution is a viable option for Christians. Indeed, without getting into the details here, I accept

---

18. Hamilton, *Seeing Gray*, 79–88.

theistic evolution as our best approach to explaining human origins.[19]

Adam Hamilton also embraces theistic evolution, and offers it as another example of seeing gray. However, committing to evolution (theistic or otherwise) is a matter of black and white, it seems to me, not gray. In my own experience, dialogue/debate on this question is not about compromise, or somehow finding middle ground between science and religion. On this topic, agreement usually comes when someone changes his or her mind.

4. Christology

The next controversy dividing liberals and conservatives and for which Adam seeks to find compromise brings us to the question of the person of Jesus.[20] Liberal Christians are described as seeing Jesus as a revolutionary, while conservative Christians emphasize Jesus as personal Savior and Lord. Essentially this can be seen as a debate between the social dimensions of salvation versus personal dimensions, or social holiness versus personal holiness.

I appreciate Adam's emphasis on holding both of these together: "It is only as we hold together both the

---

19. Bill T. Arnold, *Genesis,* New Cambridge Bible Commentary (Cambridge and New York: Cambridge University Press, 2009), 51–52.

20. Hamilton, *Seeing Gray,* 89–96.

evangelical and social gospels that we find the fullness of the good news."[21] Essentially both positions have been in error at times by overemphasizing one or the other dimension of Jesus and his mission.

On the other hand, Adam states that Jesus shared some things in common with the sects of the Judaism of his day (Essenes, Sadducees, and Pharisees), but refused to fit the mold of any one of them. The reason, according to Adam, is because these groups saw the world in black-and-white terms. Jesus, in contrast, preached a gospel that represents gray.

It's clear that Jesus didn't fit neatly into any of the sects of early Judaism. But that's hardly because he preached a gray gospel. Indeed, the central themes of Jesus' ministry were hardly gray topics: "The time is fulfilled, and the kingdom of God has come near; repent, and believe in the good news" (Mark 1:15 NRSV). And the articulation of Paul's gospel was "a scandal to Jews and foolishness to Gentiles" (1 Cor. 1:23). Both men were rejected, not because they offered gray solutions, but partly because they articulated black-and-white truths in a world of gray.

5. Universalism

Adam next takes up the question of who makes it to heaven. He says this problem, more than any other,

---

21. Hamilton, *Seeing Gray*, 95.

likely highlights the differences between conservative and liberal Christians.[22] There are two extreme positions on this point. First, *restrictivism* (Adam uses the somewhat less precise term *exclusivism*) asserts that no one goes to heaven without explicitly receiving the gospel and confessing that Jesus is Lord. Second, *universalism* teaches that all will eventually be reconciled to God and admitted into heaven, regardless of personal faith in Jesus.

Adam helpfully presents the problems with both extremes, and embraces "a middle position" between universalism and restrictivism, which he calls *inclusivism*. Such Christian inclusivism has the following features, according to Adam.[23] First, it admits that some individuals reject the grace of God, and are therefore deserving of perdition. Second, it accepts that Jesus' atoning work is the exclusive means through which God saves. Third, it maintains that salvation is by faith and not by works. Fourth, it asserts that God's saving mercy extends to many who seek him although they do not understand to call upon the name of Jesus.

In support of Christian inclusivism, Adam appeals to luminaries such as Justin Martyr, Ulrich Zwingli, John Wesley, and in more recent times, C. S. Lewis and

---

22. Hamilton, *Seeing Gray*, 97–111.
23. Ibid., 109.

John R. W. Stott, as Christians who have accepted inclusivism. To this list, we might add the statements of the Roman Catholic Church in Vatican II and the teachings of Pope Benedict XVI.[24]

Without doubt, the most influential Christian of the twentieth century on this question (and many others) was C. S. Lewis. He made the case in more than one context that salvation comes only through Jesus Christ, while overt and explicit confession of faith in this life is not essential. He believed that an individual could be a true follower of Jesus without consciously knowing it, sometimes called an "anonymous Christian." Lewis's understanding of Christian inclusivism may be summarized as follows.

> What we discover with Lewis . . . is a firm belief in a God whose primary requirement of his creatures is not epistemic precision but heart purity. Yet that does not mean all roads lead to heaven, as the universalist insists. Lewis was adamant about Christ's being the exclusive way to God. He simply argued that some people, due to infirmities or

---

24. Joseph Ratzinger, before he became Benedict XVI and with the approval of Pope John Paul II, reiterated the church's position articulated in the Second Vatican Council that God bestows salvific grace to individual non-Christians "in ways known to himself." See http://www.vatican.va/roman_curia/congregations/cfaith/documents/rc_con_cfaith_doc_20000806_dominus-iesus_en.html.

circumstances beyond their control, will never hear the gospel, or if they do, they will hear it through a tainted filter of distortion.[25]

This position is sometimes called the "Wider Hope."

I think Adam is right to explore this idea as an alternative to restrictivism and universalism. I also think Christians should continue developing this idea of the "Wider Hope" (which is more precise than the term *inclusivism*).[26] My only observation at this point in the discussion is that Christian inclusivism is not a middle-way solution found by taking the best of two extremes—universalism and restrictivism—and combining them into something new. This has been a genuine alternative for almost two thousand years, and it was not developed in the church by combining the best of two positions that can be simplistically categorized as liberal and conservative. Many Christians who are otherwise conservative have embraced the idea of the Wider Hope.

---

25. See Scott R. Burson and Jerry L. Walls, *C. S. Lewis and Francis Schaeffer: Lessons for a New Century from the Most Influential Apologists of Our Time* (Downers Grove, IL: InterVarsity Press, 1998), 212, and 211–13 for summary of Lewis generally on this point.

26. And in fact, variations of Christian inclusivism have been explored by leading theologians, such as Karl Rahner, John R. W. Stott, and many others, and continues to be considered today in a way we cannot cover briefly here.

6. Hell

Along the same lines, Adam turns to what he considers the next black-and-white controversy: the question of whether hell exists.[27] He observes that some conservatives have a literalistic view. Liberals, on the other hand, often assume a dismissive and overly optimistic view of hell, denying its existence.

Adam traces briefly the biblical evidence, and asserts simply that he rejects "the idea that there is no such place or state as hell."[28] At the same time, he warns against taking literally the metaphors and similes used to describe hell. He concludes that we should accept hell as real, not simply because of the biblical evidence but because the reality of hell seems to be a "necessary and logical corollary to heaven."[29]

---

27. Hamilton, *Seeing Gray*, 113–19.

28. Ibid., 114.

29. Ibid., 116. On hell as logical and necessary, the reader would benefit greatly from the measured and careful scholarship of Jerry L. Walls, *Hell: The Logic of Damnation* (Notre Dame: University of Notre Dame Press, 1992). Walls, a leading Christian philosopher in our Wesleyan tradition, has also authored books on heaven (*Heaven: The Logic of Eternal Joy* [New York: Oxford University Press, 2002]) and purgatory (*Purgatory: The Logic of Total Transformation* [New York: Oxford University, 2011), among many other important works related to these topics. His work represents perfectly reasonable and well-argued Wesleyan positions on hell and universalism that are neither Falwell-like nor Spong-like.

In this case, Adam's position is no third-way position at all. He clearly lands on one side of the issue—hell, he concludes, does exist. Then he calls simply for a mature and informed way of understanding the biblical evidence related to the nature of hell. In this example, he offers no genuine middle-way compromise that strengthens or reforms Christianity. His discussion is, rather, a pastoral explanation of how to read the biblical data about the existence of hell.

7. Theodicy

Next Adam turns to a problem frequently studied by theologians, the problem of "theodicy," or the attempt to explain the obvious presence of evil and suffering in a world created and governed by an all-powerful and good God.[30] After considering two of the most common answers—deism and determinism—Adam offers a third way between these extremes.

Deism accepts the existence of God, but denies that God is involved in the natural world in any way. God is an absent Creator, who has left the natural order of the universe to spin out of control. Thus, evil and suffering are the results of an absentee God. On the other hand, determinism believes that God, in his sovereignty, has predetermined everything that happens, and therefore

---

30. Hamilton, *Seeing Gray*, 121–32.

everything will eventually have a good and positive result. We cannot see or experience the goodness of all events because we lack God's perspective.

Adam rightly rejects both alternatives. He then offers what he considers a "third alternative" or a "third way."[31] He begins by asserting that God is active and involved in the world around us (against deism) but that God does not cause things to happen to innocent people (against determinism). Instead, God has given human beings freedom of action in a world in which the natural order of things sometimes leads to pain and suffering for innocent people. God does not cause bad things to happen, but God uses those bad things to bring about good in ways that surprise us.

Adam's discussion is very pastoral and helpful (he uses several illustrations). I don't disagree with his general approach. But neither is this answer a third-way solution unavailable until now. This is no gray area between black and white extremes. What Adam has described is essentially good Wesleyan theology, and has been available for centuries. God has created human beings to have a limited degree of free will in the natural order of the universe, which is necessary for love to be genuine. But freedom necessarily involves the

---

31. Hamilton, *Seeing Gray*, 122.

possibility of abuse of freedom.[32] Moreover, free will is required in order for moral accountability to be genuine ("love your neighbor," "you shall not murder," etc.). If moral virtue is to be real, humans must have the liberty to choose otherwise. Human beings without free will would be protected against falling, sin would be impossible to define, and the moral imperatives of God would be nonsensical.[33]

The Quest for the Middle Way

Adam's purpose in *Seeing Gray* is to find middle ground between Reverend Falwell and Bishop Spong. His goal is to articulate a middle way between the extremes, to give voice to a centered or balanced Christian faith that will move the church to a new reformation. This goal is

---

32. For some of what follows, see Thomas C. Oden, *Pastoral Theology: Essentials of Ministry* (San Francisco, CA: Harper & Row, 1983), 223–44, esp. 227–28. And on Libertarian freedom, see again Burson and Walls, *C. S. Lewis and Francis Schaeffer*, 67–68, and Barr, *Modern Physics and Ancient Faith*, 175–89.

33. This section of *Seeing Gray* presents two more issues, doubt and spirituality, which however do not present real debated issues or third-way compromises (chapter 15, "In Praise of Honest Doubt," 133–37; chapter 16, "The Messy Truth about Spirituality," 139–43). Adam's discussions of these are helpful and pastoral, with illustrations and inspirational quotes. But I am omitting a summary of them here because they are not relevant to the larger questions before us.

clearly explained in his introduction.[34] And throughout the discussion, he makes frequent references to the third way, middle way, or third option.

What he seeks may be technically identified as a *tertium quid*, a third thing related to two opposites typically considered the only two options available. His assumption is that each of these disputes is a conflict between two *and only two* extremes, and a middle way is sought that combines the best of both extremes. The *tertium quid* approach usually involves the idea of mixing two opposing things together, transforming them and yielding a new, unique thing.

Adam's impulse to find middle-way alternatives in all our debates has a longstanding and honored tradition in Christianity. To explain what I mean, consider an example from the early church illustrating how Christians have almost always resolved conflict. One of the greatest debates in the church more than fifteen hundred years ago was over the nature and person of Christ himself (the study of Christology). Some Christians argued that Christ had two distinct persons, divine and human, which were in harmony with each other but separate, like a mixture of oil and water mingling but not mixing (Nestorians). Other Christians believed this was heresy, and argued instead that Christ had but one person, in whom the

---

34. Hamilton, *Seeing Gray*, xiii–xvii.

divine and human were blended, the divine essentially absorbing the human (Eutychianism).

The Council of Chalcedon settled the matter in AD 451 in what has been called a "middle-of-the-road settlement." The mystery of Christ was described as one person with two natures: "the same perfect in divinity and perfect in humanity, the same truly God and truly man,"[35] both natures being perfect, the same essence ("consubstantial") with both God and humans. This is considered orthodox truth today by almost all Christians. But in AD 451, it was a compromise that satisfied neither side of the debate.

In fact, much of what we today consider to be Christian orthodoxy was worked out in a similar way in the first five centuries of the church in four "councils." The gritty, and sometimes brutal, work of the early church councils was the way the church resolved conflict and often had as much to do with power politics as it did theology (more like Vito Corleone's family business than we care to admit). Reading the story of how these early Christians worked through controversy is chilling. Sometimes they found true compromise between two positions; sometimes they devised an entirely new position—a genuine third way—which then became the new doctrine.

---

35. Diarmaid MacCulloch, *Christianity: The First Three Thousand Years* (New York: Viking, 2009), 226, and see generally 222–28.

Frankly, we shouldn't expect our current disputes to be any easier to resolve than those faced by generations of Christians before us. Or any less messy and painful. Our church, The United Methodist Church, like Christianity generally, will continue struggling with debated issues because that's what we do. As Christians, we are committed to addressing the biggest and most challenging questions of life. We will not always agree on the answers. Sometimes we will find important middle-way solutions. But sometimes we won't, and we must accept that reality. I appreciate Adam Hamilton's desire to find middle-road compromises for the church today. But what can we say about his attempt?

In nearly every one of the issues we've summarized here, Adam has failed to recognize already available options in most of these debates. This is a common mistake associated with the Fallacy of False Dilemma. He reduces each controversy to only two extremes, without asking us to consider whether there might be other options, or other coherent alternatives already available in or near the middle. After excluding those middle-way alternatives, he then proceeds to offer us a third way, a middle path to a solution. But as I have pointed out in several examples, Adam has not told you that several mediating positions are available to you, have always been there, and are perfectly reasonable alternatives to Falwell and Spong.

At times, these reasonable alternatives are long-held convictions of our Methodist forebears (for example, our view of Scripture). At others times, we have more recent Christian acceptance of ideas such as theistic evolution, which may come closer to a genuine third-way compromise. But it's altogether clear—what we have here is not anything like an agenda for reforming Christianity. And in most cases, these discussions are not genuine compromise or third-way proposals at all.

One of the problems in Adam's false dilemma is the way he lumps together conservative Christianity and fundamentalism on one side of each debated issue. On the other side stands the skeptical minimalism of liberal Christianity. These are the only options he considers before launching into his reforming proposals to offer a way forward for Christians. But those who see themselves as orthodox Wesleyan Christians have been excluded. I am not personally comfortable with "conservative Christianity" as most North American reformed denominations define it (and they're the folks who get to define these things too often). And I'm certainly not comfortable with fundamentalism, nor with liberalism. In reality, Adam sets up the controversial issues as though we don't already have answers to these questions.

But we do! The dilemma is false. As we saw at the beginning of this chapter, Adam's vision for a reformation of Christianity draws upon what he calls the best of fundamentalism and liberalism combining the evangelical and social gospels. Such Christian faith considers both the divine and human dimensions of Scripture, and exhibits both a deep personal faith in Jesus and a heart for social justice. Look no further! We have it in what we call Wesleyanism. This is what marked and characterized our early theology and heritage, and has been available to us for these two centuries as among the most important distinctives of our Methodist tradition.

The vast and roomy center, where numerous balanced and orthodox options have been made available long ago, has not been taken into consideration in Adam's approach. Then the innovative solutions he offers are not new at all. Or they are not genuine middle-way solutions at all. In some cases, Adam has simply taken a position on one side or the other, rather than forging a new middle-road solution. So, he believes for example that hell exists, clearly landing on one side of the debate.

This attempt to find a middle-road solution to all the controversial issues of our day is ultimately flawed by another critical error. The approach assumes that each issue will eventually yield a genuine tertium quid or middle-way solution. In some instances, the middle way is contrived. It just doesn't exist. And this brings me to my next subject—the fork in the road.

3

The Fork in the Road

Irrepressible American philosopher Yogi Berra is credited with saying: "When you come to a fork in the road, take it."[1]

We don't really know if the baseball great was the first to say this. Who cares?! The old adage captures something we all recognize as wonderful wisdom. The humor of the proverb works, of course, because the advice "take it" isn't very helpful. We're expecting some word of wisdom that will help us decide one way or the other, left or right, to continue along the road. Which of my two options is the most direct route to my destination? Which

---

1. He even wrote a book by that title: Yogi Berra, with Dave Kaplan, *When You Come to a Fork in the Road, Take It!: Inspiration and Wisdom from One of Baseball's Greatest Heroes* (New York: Hyperion, 2001).

is easier? Which is quicker? Most important, which will actually get me to my destination instead of turning out to be a detour down the wrong path? The humor works because the punch line "take it" is surprising. It doesn't answer any of our questions or match our expectations.

Berra's simple proverb contains two unstated premises at work in the setup line, "when you come to a fork in the road." First, it assumes we are on a road moving forward to a destination. The fork in the path presents us with a dilemma. If we want to move forward, we must decide, left or right. Sitting down in the middle of the road or turning back are not options. Or at least, these are not options that get us to our desired destination. Second, the saying assumes we only have two options before us, left or right. The fork presents no other possibilities. We can complain about this, or wish it weren't so. But the proverb assumes we have these two options only.

Perhaps The United Methodist Church can learn something from Berra's humor. Is there a middle way on the difficult issue of human sexuality? Can we find a third option? Or is it necessarily true that our church has arrived at a denominational fork in the road?

In this chapter, I invite you to consider another logical flaw with the attempt to find a middle way forward on human sexuality. The problem with the argument is that it involves an unwarranted assumption. Many such arguments are said to "beg the question," which in this case means they assume the point to be proven is true when, in fact, it hasn't been established as true.[2] Such arguments smuggle the conclusion into the premises.

So, in Adam Hamilton's approach (again, simply as an example of this argument), we are asked to believe that we should seek a middle way on the question of human sexuality because the church cannot move forward to a better future if we don't. Put another way, this argument says that if we do not find a middle way on the debate, then the church will not move forward.

There are two examples of question begging in this approach. The first is the unwarranted assumption that a middle way is *possible* between two paths. The two paths are represented by those who believe the church should ordain individuals who celebrate same-sex practices, and those who do not. The second unwarranted assumption is the idea that finding such a middle way between these positions (were it possible) would be *progress* for the church. This chapter picks up the first

---

2. Frances Howard-Snyder, Daniel Howard-Snyder, and Ryan Wasserman, *The Power of Logic*, 5th ed. (New York: McGraw-Hill, 2012), 177–88, and specifically for the fallacy of question begging, see 177–80. Begging the question is considered a circular argument, technically known by the Latin expression *petitio principii*, "begging the first principle."

assumption for your consideration, and the next two chapters consider the second.

Holiness or Hospitality

Our denomination's debate over human sexuality has continued without resolution since the 1970s. During the last two General Conferences in which I have been privileged to participate, I often heard the debate expressed in terms of two themes of the gospel: holiness versus hospitality.

Holiness. Some argue on the basis of holiness that we should not ordain individuals who celebrate same-sex practices as a God-blessed alternative lifestyle. This position accepts the current UMC statement that same-sex practices are "incompatible with Christian teaching."[3] The Scripture is consistent in its view of such practices. The history of Christianity is unanimous in this position, and in short, this is not a lifestyle that God or God's people can endorse.

Christ invites us to enter into a loving and forgiven relationship with him. We are invited to come "just as we are," but Christ doesn't leave us where we are. The

---

3. *The Book of Discipline of The United Methodist Church 2012* (Nashville, TN: The United Methodist Publishing House, 2012), 111, ¶161F.

love of Christ seeks the best for us, a life of holy *shalom*, otherwise understood as "life to the fullest" offered by Christ (John 10:10). Christian teaching is clear that same-sex practices are not God's best for us. The UMC should strive to find new ways to affirm "that all persons are individuals of sacred worth,"[4] including new ways to welcome, love, forgive, and serve one another, yet we should nevertheless not endorse same-sex practices or ordain candidates for ministry who accept and celebrate a same-sex lifestyle.[5] To do so would be to accept less than God's best design for the church and less than God's best plan for our lives individually.

Those in this camp believe the debate on this topic is driven and influenced by changes in contemporary culture. Such cultural currents are not normative for the church and should not determine how the church thinks about human sexuality. The conclusion: on the basis of holy character—both God's and ours—the UMC should maintain its current position against same-sex practices.

Hospitality. Others argue that Christianity is characterized first and foremost by love, as exemplified by Christ. On the basis of Christ's unconditional love, we should change the UMC position on same-sex practices

---

4. *Book of Discipline*, 111, ¶161F.

5. Ibid., 200, ¶304.3

in order to welcome all who seek ordination into full inclusion in the life of the church. This is a justice issue. The love of Christ constrains us to name the current UMC position on same-sex practices as discriminatory.

The Scripture has precious little to say about this issue. Jesus nowhere mentions homosexuality. The Bible has only about five verses on it, and those references are embedded in ancient Near Eastern and Greco-Roman cultural specifics. The interpretation of those verses is up for debate and hardly settles the issue. Moreover, the church has a long history of using the Bible to treat people unjustly, such as race-based slavery and the repression of women. This is just another example of the way the church has failed to defend the helpless or fight for the rights of those who live outside the ranks of power, or "acceptable society."

Christ calls us to a life of loving *shalom*, which is enhanced when people learn to accept themselves for who they are. The church should not discriminate against anyone because of whom they love. The ministry of the UMC is hurt by this unjust stance, which is driving our youth to other, inclusive denominations. We will only reach God's best for our church and for us individually when we acknowledge and welcome all into full inclusion into the life of the church. The conclusion: on the basis of Christ's love, the UMC should change its current stance against same-sex practices.

So there you have it in a nutshell—holiness versus hospitality. Before we go any further, I need to warn you that this is an overly simplistic way to frame the argument. Thinking about the debate in this way is catchy, like sound bites in a political debate. But also like sound bites, such arguments are superficial and inadequate. They don't get us very far.

Our entrenchment into two easily summarized camps also makes it too easy to attack each other. People who frame the debate in terms of hospitality tend to object that the other side unfairly labels homosexuality as incompatible with Christian teaching while going silent on racism, sexism, heterosexual sin, or the abuse of power and money. Where is the holiness in that? On the other hand, people who frame the debate in terms of holiness object that the other side is not serious about Scripture, the two-thousand-year-tradition of Christianity, or the nature of saving faith itself. How can Christian faith be reduced so nimbly to nothing more than hospitality?

I will return to this way of understanding the debate in chapter 5. Essentially, I will make the case there that holiness is really central to who we are as Christians and to Christian truth. This is a theological tenet. Hospitality, on the other hand, is a Christian virtue. Pitting the two against each other as a way of framing our debate is a category mistake, and doesn't get us very far.

For now, it is important to acknowledge that, for all the inadequacies of this way of framing the arguments, there is a certain degree of truth in focusing on these two topics—holiness and hospitality. These appear to be our only options. The rest of this chapter invites you to consider with me the sad reality that we as a church really are at a stalemate. And I turn now to the very thing that drives the fork in our road, dividing us into two paths: the way we read Scripture.

Reading the Bible the Wesley Way

In my brief descriptions of the two options before us—holiness or hospitality—you will notice that both sides appeal to Scripture to defend their arguments. The holiness argument holds that the Bible is consistent in its condemnation of same-sex practices. The hospitality approach holds that the few references in the Bible on this topic are inconclusive and irrelevant. The few references here and there are not enough to settle the issue, it is argued. And besides, they say, the overarching themes of Scripture drive us to welcome everyone regardless of sexual practices.

And so next we need to explore the role of the Bible in this debate. Those who argue for changing the UMC position on same-sex practices often make two assertions. First, they typically emphasize how few references there are in the Bible to homosexuality.[6] Adam Hamilton is again our example in this approach. His chapter in *Seeing Gray* on "Homosexuality at the Center" is essentially the manuscript of a sermon he preached on the subject for his congregation (the sermon itself is on pages 168–85).[7] He sets out in the sermon to cover biblical passages that mention "anything approximating homosexual acts," even telling his congregation they are now familiar with "*every* passage" mentioning it (emphasis his). These include seven passages, four from the Old Testament and three from the New Testament.[8] Without getting into the specifics of the way Adam handles these texts, my point here is to illustrate that many people emphasize just how little the Bible actually says about same-sex practices. The implication is simple: homosexuality is

---

6. Of course, we ought to point out here that the term "homosexuality" is of relatively recent origin, made popular by German-speaking psychologists of the nineteenth century as part of their project to classify all human personality types. The term itself does not occur in the Bible. The ancient world had no such abstract category for same-sex practices, while both the ancient Near Eastern and Greco-Roman worlds were well aware of such practices. Only the Bible attaches a moral prohibition against those practices.

7. Adam Hamilton, *Seeing Gray in a World of Black and White: Thoughts on Religion, Morality, and Politics* (Nashville, TN: Abingdon Press, 2008), 165–87.

8. Gen. 19:1–29; Lev. 18:22; 20:13; Judg. 19; Rom. 1:23–27; 1 Cor. 6:9–10; and 1 Tim. 1:10. He adds two additional texts in a footnote for the book, which he says he should have mentioned in the sermon: 2 Pet. 2:6–10 and Jude 7.

just not important to the biblical authors, and therefore shouldn't be an issue for us.

The second assertion one often hears by those using the hospitality argument is that all the biblical prohibitions against same-sex practices are limited to the Old Testament or the New Testament epistles. In other words, there is nothing in the four Gospels on this topic, and more to the point, Jesus himself never mentions it. This argument sometimes comes with a statement about Jesus as the final culmination, the end game of divine revelation, and therefore more authoritative than the Old Testament references or Paul's letters. Once again, the implication is clear. References that condemn same-sex practices have been countered and made irrelevant by the message of Jesus, which promotes loving acceptance of all people.

Now on the one hand, it would be easy to counter this argument by pointing out that Jesus' silence on any given subject is no tacit approval of that subject. Jesus also didn't mention genocide or rape. To argue that his silence on these topics means he approves them is of course nonsense. Nor does Jesus say anything about nuclear proliferation. I mention this one because we all understand that nuclear proliferation is a much later development. Jesus didn't mention it because it didn't yet exist. I will explain in chapter 6 that homosexuality as an objectified concept didn't yet exist in the first century

AD. Jesus certainly knew of same-sex practices, and it's likely he at least shared the widespread assumption of the Greco-Roman world around him that such practices were a sexual aberration. Given his reliance on the Old Testament texts, it seems even more likely he would have identified same-sex practices as wrong.

That would be the easy way of responding to the argument that Jesus was silent on same-sex practices. But in fact, both of these two arguments—that there are so few explicit references in the Bible to same-sex practices and that Jesus nowhere mentions the topic—expose much deeper problems with the way the hospitality argument reads the Bible. Such arguments are so fundamentally flawed in the way the Bible is used in the debate, no simple point-by-point refutation is enough. Here instead I offer three principles of interpretation that are desperately needed in the debate among United Methodists. These three progress from the simplest to the most complex, and in the case of the third principle, the most important for Wesleyans.

1. Texts in Contexts—As United Methodists, we insist on taking "individual texts in light of their place in the Bible as a whole."[9] This is our statement against what is commonly called "proof-texting," or lifting a single verse from somewhere in the Bible, stripping it of its

---

9. *2012 Book of Discipline*, 82, ¶105.

surrounding literary context, and using it to prove what it never intended to support.[10] For example, by proof-texting, one could argue that the Old Testament psalmist is an atheist because he says "There is no God" (Ps. 14:1). But of course, in reality, the whole line reads: "Fools say in their hearts, There is no God." The argument makes the psalmist say just the opposite of what the whole psalm is actually teaching.

Now on this point, both sides of our current debate are guilty of abusing the Bible. Some argue against approval of same-sex practices by simply appealing to Leviticus 18:22: "You must not have sexual inter-course with a man as you would with a woman; it is a detestable practice." That seems to settle the issue. But others rightly point out that the Old Testament law has several other such texts with quite specific prohibitions. For example, the Israelite law forbids beard-trimming (Lev. 19:27), lobster-eating (Lev. 11:10; Deut. 14:10), and a host of others. And this is not to mention the many laws requiring the reader to do something positively, such as elaborate instructions for offering animal sacrifices in worship (Lev. 1–7), or keeping the Sabbath on Saturday

---

10. In addition to literary context, we also must take each verse carefully in its linguistic and historical context; see Moisés Silva, *Biblical Words and Their Meaning: An Introduction to Lexical Semantics,* rev. and expanded ed. (Grand Rapids, MI: Zondervan, 1994), 138–48.

(Exod. 20:8–11; Deut. 5:12–15). What right do we have to choose this Old Testament law (the ban on same-sex practices), while ignoring all the others?

The implication is clear. If we wish to apply the Old Testament's ban on same-sex practices, then all these others would need applying too. And besides, the same prohibition I just quoted from Leviticus 18:22 is repeated a few chapters later, this time with the punishment required: "If a man has sexual intercourse with a man as he would with a woman, the two of them have done something detestable. They must be executed; their blood is on their own heads" (Lev. 20:13). One cannot have it both ways. Either we apply all or none of the Israelite laws, it is argued, and since none of us wants all of it, then the whole is irrelevant to the argument.

But there is a flip side to this interpretive principle against proof-texting. Yes, it's insufficient to argue against same-sex practices solely on the basis of the two prohibitions in Leviticus. But it's just as insufficient to argue that those prohibitions are irrelevant because other commands in the same context are no longer applicable to today's Christians. This is a form of reverse proof-texting. This approach isolates specific prohibitions in Leviticus (against beard-trimming or lobster-eating, for example), strips them of their contexts, and lifts them as examples of why we cannot accept the laws of Leviticus as having anything to do with us today. If we are free to trim our beards and eat lobster, as we clearly are, then implicitly we are also free to endorse same-sex practices. By denying the relevance of these proof-texts, we are told the Old Testament's understanding of human sexuality in general is also irrelevant.[11]

But this approach to the Old Testament law will not do. Let us not forget that the heart of Israelite law was summarized by Jesus as love of God and neighbor (Matt. 22:37–39; Deut. 6:4–5 and Lev. 19:18). Moreover, Jesus came into the world not to abolish the Old Testament law but to fill it up with significance (Matt. 5:17). Anyone who ignores the least one of these commandments is least in the kingdom of heaven (5:19). The way we understand the Old Testament as Christian Scripture is clearly complicated.[12] The Hebrew Scriptures were God's message and God's will for the Israelites in their time and place, and as Christian Scripture, the Old

---

11. I am only dealing here with the legal portions of the Pentateuch. The ideal definition of marriage as between one man and one woman (Gen. 2:24–25) will be a topic for the next chapter.

12. For summary and references to more reading on this important topic, see Joel B. Green, *Seized by Truth: Reading the Bible as Scripture* (Nashville, TN: Abingdon Press, 2007), 34–41. For a nuanced understanding of the Old Testament law in Christian ethics, see Christopher J. H. Wright, *Old Testament Ethics for the People of God* (Downers Grove, IL: InterVarsity Press, 2004), 314–25; and Bruce C. Birch, *Let Justice Roll Down: The Old Testament, Ethics, and Christian Life* (Louisville, KY: Westminster/John Knox Press, 1991), 157–72.

Testament's central tenets cannot be dismissed easily today, including the hard-to-understand legal portions. Proof-texting must be avoided by all parties in the debate.

Our Articles of Religion, one of the UMC's four "Doctrinal Standards," may be of some help on this question. Regarding the Old Testament, and specifically the ancient Israelite law, we have the following position.

> Although the law given from God to Moses as touching ceremonies and rites doth not bind Christians, nor ought the civil precepts thereof of necessity be received in any commonwealth; yet notwithstanding, no Christian whatsoever is free from the obedience of the commandments which are called moral.[13]

This distinction between Mosaic laws that are ceremonial, civil, and moral cannot be applied to specific laws, as some have tried. Shall we take the Ten Commandments as moral, dismissing the rest as ceremonial or civil? That won't work because the command to keep the Sabbath (Exod. 20:8–11; Deut. 5:12–15) is moral, ceremonial, *and* civil. So while these categories cannot be applied specifically to individual verses (in proof-texting fashion), they are helpful nonetheless in understanding the way the Old Testament is still God's *word* for Christians today while not necessarily representing God's *command* to us

---

13. *2012 Book of Discipline*, 65, ¶105, Article VI.

in every instance. We therefore are compelled to look for principles and truths lying beneath the surface of each command, and in case-by-case fashion, look for ways these truths are relevant for our edification today.

In this way, even the prohibitions against beard-trimming and lobster-eating contribute to our understanding of the way ancient Israelites were to relate to Yahweh their holy God as a holy people. The immediate context in each case explains that the prohibitions are related to living a holy life before God (lobster-eating = Lev. 11:44–45; beard-trimming = Lev.19:2 and Deut. 14:2). In a similar way, the laws against sexual impurities (not only same-sex practices, but laws against bestiality, incest, and others) contributed to the Israelite understanding of living in a covenant relationship with a holy God. We may try to argue that those prohibitions are culturally embedded in ancient stigmas or outmoded in light of today's advanced views, and therefore apply only in some indirect fashion. But we cannot dismiss them as altogether irrelevant to the debate.

2. The Canon of Scripture—As United Methodists, we view the Bible as "sacred canon for Christian people," specifically the "thirty-nine books of the Old Testament and the twenty-seven books of the New Testament."[14] As sacred canon (or authoritative standard) for the church,

---

14. *2012 Book of Discipline*, 82, ¶105.

we believe the Bible is not primarily inspired for us to know *things* (epistemology). We learn quite a lot from the Bible, of course. But this is not its primary function *in and for the church*. Instead, the Bible is inspired and given by God to the church in order for Christians to know God through personal and corporate salvation (soteriology).[15] Even my use of the word "know" in the previous sentences has different meanings. By "know" when referring to things, I'm essentially referring to the use of my brain to accumulate facts. But by "know" when referring to God, I mean encountering God and relating to him in a way made possible by the sacrificial atonement of Christ on the cross. We believe the whole canon is a gift from God, inspired to lead us to an intimate relationship with God individually and corporately, and to transform us into God's image, individually and corporately.

On the canonical unity of the sixty-six books of the Bible, we stand squarely on the shoulders of our forebear, John Wesley, whose view of Scripture underscored its authority and inspiration. He constantly spoke

---

15. Kenneth J. Collins, *The Evangelical Moment: The Promise of an American Religion* (Grand Rapids, MI: Baker Academic, 2005), 70–78. For more on reading the Scripture soteriologically rather than epistemologically, see William J. Abraham, "Scripture and Divine Revelation," in *Wesley, Wesleyans, and Reading the Bible as Scripture,* ed. Joel B. Green and David F. Watson (Waco, TX: Baylor University Press, 2012), 117–32.

of "the whole Scripture," "the whole tenor of Scripture," and "the general tenor of Scripture," as ways of emphasizing the wholeness and unity of the Bible.[16] As part of our theological task, the Bible functions with a single purpose (wholeness) and is consistent and coherent (unity).

Wesley shared with other interpreters of the seventeenth and eighteenth centuries an emphasis on "the analogy of faith," as a means of highlighting its unity, consistency, and authority for faith and practice. For example, in arguing against the Calvinist understanding of "double predestination," which teaches that God unconditionally saves some and damns others, Wesley objected that such a doctrine is contrary to "the whole scope and tenor of Scripture" as well as specific passages like "God is love."[17] Without going into detail here, I will use the words of Bishop Scott Jones to summarize a genuinely Wesleyan understanding of Scripture, which at least includes the following.

> [A Wesleyan understanding of Scripture] would seek
> the whole message of the Bible, listening carefully to

---

16. Scott J. Jones, *John Wesley's Conception and Use of Scripture* (Nashville: Kingswood Books, 1995), 43–53 and 219–21.

17. "Free Grace," *The Sermons of John Wesley: A Collection for the Christian Journey,* ed. Kenneth J. Collins and Jason E. Vickers (Nashville, TN: Abingdon Press, 2013), 26, ¶20.

its individual parts but also seeking to understand the entire book as concerning the saving activity of God, reconciling humanity to himself and restoring them to the image in which they were created.[18]

In our interpretive tradition as Wesleyans, we do not elevate one portion or sub-portion of the Bible as more authoritative than others. There is a certain progression or gradual revealing of God and God's message in the Bible. But we do not believe that later stages of revelation necessarily replace, dismiss, or nullify earlier stages of revelation (known as supersessionism). We accept no hierarchal structure of one portion of the canon over against others. The words of Jesus do not somehow trump the words of Paul and Moses, or Jeremiah and Peter, or for that matter, the anonymous authors of 1–2 Samuel or 1–2 Kings. That is a simplistic way of reading the Bible and foreign to our Wesleyan tradition.

One unfortunate practice of some publishers is the printing of "red-letter editions" of the Bible, highlighting in red the words of Jesus. Among other problems with this practice is the issue of where the words of Jesus trail off and the words of the gospel author pick up. For example, does the speech of Jesus in John 3 end at verse 15 or verse 22? The familiar words, "God so loved the

---

18. Jones, *Conception and Use of Scripture*, 223.

world that he gave his only Son," may be commentary written by the gospel writer rather than the words of Jesus. But we believe it doesn't matter. The whole has been inspired by God for the edification of the church. Then of course, we also have God speaking from the throne in heaven at the end of the whole canon. The same Lord who said "I'm making all things new" and "I am the Alpha and the Omega" also said, "The cowardly, the faithless, the vile, the murderers, those who commit sexual immorality, those who use drugs and cast spells, the idolaters and all liars—their share will be in the lake that burns with fire and sulfur" (Rev. 21:5–8). Even if we limited our theological task to the red-letter words of Jesus and the speeches of God in the New Testament, we would still have difficult questions to address.

The point, of course, is that it's not a Methodist way of reading the Scripture to suggest the teachings of Jesus trump other authors of the Bible.[19] Yes, Jesus is the final culmination of God's revelation, the best and fullest picture of the nature of God. At the same time,

---

19. Christopher Seitz criticizes similar attempts in the Anglican communion that trump one portion of the canon with supposed readings from Jesus or Paul, essentially turning Scripture into a historical witness which can be superseded by the superior wisdom of today's church; Christopher R. Seitz, *The Character of Christian Scripture: The Significance of a Two-Testament Bible* in Studies in Theological Interpretation Series (Grand Rapids, MI: Baker, 2011).

we only come to understand that revelation because of the inspiration of the oracles of God given in the canon of Scripture—both Old and New Testaments—for our edification.

3. The Primacy of Scripture—As United Methodists, we are convinced "that Scripture is the primary source and criterion for Christian doctrine."[20] In this conviction we again stand squarely on the shoulders of our forebear, John Wesley, who embraced the Protestant theological principle of *sola Scriptura*—that is, in "Scripture alone" is all knowledge necessary for salvation and holiness. While Wesley took Scripture as "the only and sufficient rule both of Christian faith and practice," he also turned to other authorities to confirm and develop his understanding of the message of Scripture.[21]

Specifically Wesley recognized five authorities for Christian doctrine, while never losing sight of Scripture

---

20. *2012 Book of Discipline*, 81, ¶105.

21. John Wesley, "The Character of a Methodist," in *The Works of John Wesley*, ed. Thomas Jackson, 3rd ed., 14 vols. (London: Wesleyan Methodist Book Room, 1872; repr. Grand Rapids, MI: Baker Book House, 1978), vol. 8, 339–47, esp. 340, ¶1. While Wesley's acceptance of *sola Scriptura* is hardly in question, his understanding is complex and distinct from that of earlier Reformers, as it should be and as the following discussion will show; cf. William J. Abraham, *Canon and Criterion in Christian Theology from the Fathers to Feminism* (Oxford: Oxford University Press, 1998), 147–61.

as primary among them.[22] *Scripture* and *reason* are a type of joint authority in that reason serves to supplement and interpret Scripture. A third authority for Wesley was *Christian antiquity*, or the "primitive church," by which he means Christianity before Emperor Constantine in the fourth century AD. Wesley believed doctrines should be proved by Scripture and reason, and by early church history if need be. Fourth was the *Church of England*, in which Wesley was an ordained priest. He turned specifically to the church's liturgy, articles of religion, and homilies, although he was clear that its authority was subordinate to Scripture. The fifth and last source of authority for Wesley was *experience*, by which he primarily means specifically Christian experience. This criterion for Christian doctrine is least of all. Whenever Wesley sees instances where Scripture and experience deviate, he characterizes Scripture as trustworthy and experience as untrustworthy. In sum, "no one who reads Wesley carefully could possibly miss the primacy of Scripture over the others."[23]

---

22. For some of what follows on these five authorities, see Jones, *Conception and Use of Scripture*, 62–103. For convenient summary of John Wesley on the primacy of Scripture, see Thomas C. Oden, *John Wesley's Teachings, Volume 1: God and Providence* (Grand Rapids, MI: Zondervan, 2012), 65–79.

23. Jones, *Conception and Use of Scripture*, 64.

This historical overview of Wesley's use of five authorities has been reduced and crystalized in the UMC in the so-called Methodist quadrilateral: Scripture, tradition (combining the early church with the Church of England), experience, and reason.[24] Albert Outler first used the term "quadrilateral" and subsequently regretted its use, although he defended the approach as accurately describing Wesley's method.[25] In 1985, he summarized his thoughts as follows.

> The term "quadrilateral" does not occur in the Wesley corpus—and more than once, I have regretted having coined it for contemporary use, since it has been so widely misconstrued.[26]

Unfortunately, our language of four "resources for theological understanding" is unclear and introduces confusion in our debates. The quadrilateral is not a

---

24. *2012 Book of Discipline*, 80–86, ¶105; I am following William J. Abraham in using "Methodist quadrilateral" rather than "Wesleyan quadrilateral" to avoid the impression that other branches of the Wesleyan family necessarily have the same understanding, not to mention to avoid the dispute of whether or not such a fourfold approach can really be traced to John Wesley; William J. Abraham, *Waking from Doctrinal Amnesia: The Healing of Doctrine in The United Methodist Church* (Nashville, TN: Abingdon Press, 1995), 108n9.

25. Albert C. Outler, "The Wesleyan Quadrilateral—In John Wesley," *Wesleyan Theological Journal* 20 (1985): 7–18.

26. Ibid., 16.

theological doctrine; it's merely a way of describing a thoughtful way of doing theology. By emphasizing the primacy of Scripture, our Wesleyan tradition means we turn to the other three elements of the quadrilateral (reason, tradition, and experience) for help *when interpreting Scripture.* They are privileged in the process hermeneutically (as instruments for interpreting the Bible) but not epistemologically (as sources for truth). They are useful norms for interpreting Scripture, not as independent sources in theology.[27]

We have committed ourselves to a geometric metaphor for the way we do theology. It is at least an indelicate use of geometry as a way of explaining how we Methodists use these authorities to develop our theology. And it is especially unhelpful where it has been used to imply an equality among the four elements. I agree with Don Thorsen that no geometric figure is adequate to explain Wesley's approach. If we insist on choosing one, perhaps it would have been better to use a tetrahedron (a tetrahedral pyramid), in which Scripture serves as the foundation of a pyramid, while reason, tradition, and

---

27. For this distinction, see William J. Abraham, "Scripture and Divine Revelation," 118; and Jerry L. Walls, *The Problem of Pluralism: Recovering United Methodist Identity* (Wilmore, KY: Good News Books, 1986), 80–86.

experience appear as its three sides, as complementary but not primary sources of religious authority.[28]

It could be said of the UMC that the reason we talk about how many sources we use in *doing theology* is because we cannot agree on *having a theology*. This is almost certainly true of the origins of the Methodist quadrilateral. William J. Abraham has shown that the UMC formed in 1968 could not resolve tension between its doctrinal heritage and its process for theological reflection. As a result, our church defined itself by the way we do theology rather than in what we believe doctrinally.

> Process took precedence over content. United Methodist identity was located not in the content of what one believed but in the process of how one came to believe. . . . What made one a United Methodist from a doctrinal point of view was a clear commitment to developing those doctrines which could be supported in an appropriate way by Scripture, tradition, reason, and experience.[29]

---

28. Don Thorsen, *The Wesleyan Quadrilateral: Scripture, Tradition, Reason & Experience as a Model of Evangelical Theology* (Lexington, KY: Emeth Press, 1990), 38.

29. Abraham, *Waking from Doctrinal Amnesia*, 45. The same conclusion could be drawn from reading the summary in W. Stephen Gunter et al., *Wesley and the Quadrilateral: Renewing the Conversation* (Nashville, TN: Abingdon Press, 1997), 9–10.

Instead of establishing church doctrine, the 1972 General Conference created a way of thinking about doctrine. On the one hand, since the 1988 General Conference, we have been clear that our doctrinal distinctives are found in four foundational documents: (a) the Articles of Religion of the Methodist Church, (b) the Confession of Faith of the Evangelical United Brethren Church, (c) the *Standard Sermons* of Wesley, and (d) Wesley's *Explanatory Notes upon the New Testament*.[30] And we have a long and robust history of "practical divinity" in which we emphasize the realization of the gospel in the lives of Christian people.[31] On the other hand, too many of us see these documents as merely "historical roots" of Methodism rather than doctrinal standards. If we look upon these standards as merely quaint expressions of an older Methodism, we are certainly left without a full-bodied theology to guide our church.

At the end of the day, this geometric metaphor (the "quadrilateral") is a central feature of our current debates over human sexuality. The use of tradition can be confusing, because Wesley himself did not have many nice things to say about the history of Christianity, especially as a source or norm for doing theology. As we have seen, tradition in his theological method was

---

30. *2012 Book of Discipline*, 63–75, ¶104.

31. Ibid., 49–54, ¶102.

largely limited to the first three centuries of Christianity, supplemented by the doctrines of the Church of England as held in Wesley's day.

Similarly experience can be misleading. In his own practice of interpreting the Bible, Wesley often turned to an awareness of God's presence in the lives of individuals in the early Methodist movement for help. In particular, he was interested in hearing testimonies of those giving witness to an assurance of salvation by faith. Outler refers to Wesley's "special genius" in adding "experience" to the traditional Anglican triad of Scripture, reason, and tradition, in order "to incorporate the notion of conversion into the Anglican tradition."[32] Especially after his own heart-warming experience at Aldersgate Street, Wesley was seeking a way to legitimize his own conversion experience and those of others into the Anglican way of doing theology. But this is very different from the way experience is often used in our current debate.

Scripture Versus Experience?

As we have seen, experience in Wesley's method plays a confirming role, intending to clarify his interpretation of Scripture, which always remained primary. As Outler put it:

---

32. Outler, "Quadrilateral," 10–11.

> Christian experience adds nothing to the substance of Christian truth; its distinctive role is to energize the heart so as to enable the believer to speak and do the truth in love.[33]

Yet in our current debate on human sexuality, experience in the quadrilateral has come to mean something else. It is commonplace in our debate today to hear the hospitality argument appealing to the witness of fellow Christians who embrace and celebrate their same-sex attractions in ways that are perceived to be faithful and responsible. Their experiences are perceived as theological evidence for correcting the Bible or the traditions of the church on homosexuality.

This is one way in which the Methodist quadrilateral has been "widely misconstrued" (to borrow Outler's phrase). Wesley added experience to the three sources of the Church of England (Scripture, reason, and tradition) in order to take into account specifically the Christian experience of conversion: "the vital Christian experience of the assurance of one's sins forgiven."[34] He was most interested in *Christian* experience, not common human experiences. This understanding of experience as a way of confirming the interpretation of Scripture may be summarized as follows.

---

33. Outler, "Quadrilateral," 10.
34. Ibid., 9.

> General human experience is important evidence in
> many matters of fact. For theological issues, it is only
> the Christian experience of real believers that counts.[35]

The hospitality argument for "full inclusion" makes of "experience" something never intended by Wesley or Outler, and not supported by our Wesleyan tradition. No matter how much we may like an individual, or consider that individual a good and decent person, his or her sexual experiences are not of equal value with Scripture or the traditions of the church when sorting out our church's teaching on human sexuality.

Our debate on this issue puts one piece of the quadrilateral in conflict with another, often Scripture versus experience. In Adam Hamilton's case, he is convinced by the scriptural evidence.

> I believe the Bible clearly teaches that God's design
> for marriage is heterosexuality and that there is
> something important about the male and female
> complementing each other, not simply physiologi-
> cally, but also emotionally and spiritually.[36]

At the same time, he acknowledges that some people, the approximately 5 percent who self-identify as gay or lesbian, "do not fit the norm of Scripture." But this

---

35. Jones, *Conception and Use of Scripture*, 217.
36. Hamilton, *Seeing Gray*, 186.

conflict between Scripture and experience (granting for the sake of argument one's sexual practices as normative) raises an important question.

Who of us is beyond the norm of Scripture? Does Scripture teach that human sexuality should be expressed and experienced in healthy monogamous heterosexual relationships, as Adam seems to accept? If so, then who of us can presume to live in a way other than that norm, and expect it to be a blessed and healthy relationship? How can we encourage others to live outside that norm? Certainly we are wrong to identify same-sex practices as more hurtful or unacceptable than heterosexual failures (or for that matter, racism, sexism, greed, or any number of behaviors that fall short of the norm of Scripture). I will return to the question of the norm of Scripture in the next chapter.

In conclusion, let's now return to the simple proverb: "When you come to a fork in the road, take it." As I said before, one of the premises of this wisdom is that we only have these two options, left or right. There is no third way, in the assumption of this proverb.

In Adam Hamilton's attempt to find a third alternative beyond the holiness-or-hospitality deadlock, he begs the question of whether such a third way is possible. He assumes a middle-way solution is possible on every issue about which there is controversy. But that's a logical fallacy. In this case, there simply is no third way.

In point of fact, Adam's conclusion on homosexuality in *Seeing Gray* does not offer a third way at all.[37] He agonizes over the complexity of the problem, as we all do. He calls for grace and ministry to all hurting and broken people, which is essentially our current UMC position. I do not disagree at all. The question before the church today is whether we will endorse and celebrate same-sex practices, ordain ministers who self-identify as gay or lesbian, and allow our ministers to perform same-sex weddings. Deciding to do so is not forging a new path or finding a third way. It is simply choosing one of the two paths before us. Is it right? That's a matter for all of us to ponder prayerfully, as we turn in the next chapter to the question of whether such a change is preferable for the UMC.

---

37. Hamilton, *Seeing Gray*, 183–87.

4

Promises and Pitfalls of Compromise

If you have stayed with me so far, you know that I am unconvinced by Adam Hamilton's attempt to find a third-way, middle-road Christianity. I have challenged the idea that all controversial issues can somehow be lumped together and considered collectively just because they are controversial. I have also questioned whether a new, improved, and more appealing version of Christianity would somehow appear if we could only push through our debates to find some sort of tertium quid. On the contrary, I have explained that Adam's approach fails to recognize the vast and roomy middle already occupied by The United Methodist Church. Our Wesleyan tradition has long ago provided satisfying answers to many of the controversies he thinks divide us.

On the other hand, we are at a crossroads on the question of same-sex practices. While Adam has ignored the middle choices in a false dilemma generally, it's nevertheless true that we are polarized on this issue. I have pointed out certain critical logical errors with Adam's approach of looking for a third way between the UMC's holiness-or-hospitality deadlock. The approach begs the question whether such a third way is possible. Sometimes we simply stand at a fork in the road. There is no sense complaining or crying over it. We have only two choices before us.

Here I take up the question from a different angle. Having stayed with me so far, you may now object: "Sometimes we Christians simply have to forge ahead in a new direction! Assuming we are at such a fork in the road, perhaps we must cut a new path where one doesn't already exist. Chart new territory, in order to move forward to our destination." That may certainly be true in some cases. And the church is sometimes called upon to lead the way in finding a third path as part of her prophetic ministry in the world. Is that true on the question of same-sex practices?

Let's assume for the sake of our discussion in this chapter that, in fact, a middle way *is* possible on the issue of same-sex practices. Taking Adam's approach, let's assume we can take the best of both holiness and hospitality, and combine them into a new perspective.

Once again, I believe this assumption begs the question, but this time it's a different question. Instead of asking whether or not such a middle way is *possible*, this time Adam has failed to consider whether such a middle way is *preferable*.

Remember that begging the question involves unwarranted assumptions. The question here is whether a middle-way solution on same-sex practices, if one could be found, would be preferable for the church. Preferability hasn't been proven but merely assumed to be true. The approach begs the question whether such a middle way would be favorable, whether it would necessarily be better than either of our two current options (holiness or hospitality), or more important, whether it would be always right.

On this point, the question arises whether there are times the third way is nothing more than a compromise, in the worst sense of that term. The term *compromise* has both positive and negative meanings. It can refer to a settlement of differences in which both sides make concessions, sometimes combining qualities of two differing ideas. But the concession can also be a negative or hurtful yielding of one's ideals, an accommodation of one's principles for the sake of agreement.[1] There are times when a "third way" is nothing more than a

---

1. *Oxford English Dictionary*, 2nd ed., s.v. "compromise."

compromise in this negative meaning: a surrendering of one's principles or convictions. Certainly all of us would agree in our current debate over same-sex practices that we want to avoid third-way solutions that are really only compromises in this worst sense of that term.

That is what we want to explore in this chapter. To begin, we return once more to the message of Scripture.

Scripture, Again

In the previous chapter, I explained that the norm of Scripture must be primary in our theological reflection on human sexuality, or any other question. We United Methodists turn to Scripture as our primary source of doing theology, but we also understand the supplementary role of reason, tradition, and experience in the task of interpreting Scripture.

In addition, we understand that none of us is beyond the standard or rule of Scripture, that which we called the norm of Scripture in the previous chapter. Where our experiences and practices are outside the teachings of Scripture, we pray for grace and strength to change our experiences and practices in order to live within that norm. That is our calling as Christians. That is our commitment as Methodists.

Having explained the Wesley Way of reading the Bible in the previous chapter, I turn now to explore again what the Bible says about same-sex practices in order to explain why we have such different conclusions. If we can agree that the Bible is consistently opposed to same-sex practices, how can we be so deeply divided over this issue? The answer, as you will see, is because we fail to understand the task of applying the message of the Bible to our day.

As we saw earlier, what Scripture teaches on this issue is what drives a fork in the road, dividing us into two paths. And there can hardly be any question about the specifics of what Scripture teaches. When we reviewed Adam Hamilton's survey of what the Bible teaches about same-sex practices, we noted his use of four passages from the Old Testament and three from the New Testament.[2] And we explained that it isn't adequate to discount these references simply because there are so few of them or because none of them are in the four Gospels as the words of Jesus.

Beyond these explicit prohibitions of same-sex practices, we must not neglect the refrain throughout Scripture that emphasizes God's intention in creating male and female for each other and the consistent affirmation that sexual desires rightly find fulfillment only in

---

2. Gen. 19:1–29; Lev. 18:22; 20:13; Judg. 19; Rom. 1:23–27; 1 Cor. 6:9–10; and 1 Tim. 1:10, which he then expanded to include 2 Pet. 2:6–10 and Jude 7.

heterosexual marriage.[3] Perhaps most important to this refrain is ancient Israel's ideal for marriage, which is a model for all marriages, and is embedded in creation itself (Gen. 2:24): "This is the reason that a man leaves his father and mother and embraces his wife, and they become one flesh." This indeed is the goal to which the creation story of Genesis 2 has been building, and describes the natural and God-given consequences of the male-female relationship. Marriage in ancient Israel was not perceived as the culmination of romantic love or even family commitment only, but was a mysterious and almost mystical reuniting of two parts of one sexual whole ("This one finally is bone from my bones and flesh from my flesh," 2:23). The power of sexual love is explained in the common fleshly bond that male and female had from the beginning. They belong to each other in a way that defines what it is to be human and distinguishes them from the animals.[4]

---

3. Mark 10:2–9; 1 Thess. 4:3–8; 1 Cor. 7:1–9; and others. For helpful survey and discussion, see Richard B. Hays, *The Moral Vision of the New Testament: Community, Cross, New Creation: A Contemporary Introduction to New Testament Ethics* (San Francisco, CA: HarperSanFrancisco, 1996), 390. For full scholarly treatment of both testaments, see Robert A. J. Gagnon, *The Bible and Homosexual Practice: Texts and Hermeneutics* (Nashville, TN: Abingdon Press, 2001).

4. Bill T. Arnold, *Genesis*, New Cambridge Bible Commentary (Cambridge and New York: Cambridge University Press, 2009), 61.

Jesus confirmed and strengthened this image of heterosexual marriage as God's intent for human relationships. When asked for his views on divorce, Jesus quoted Genesis 1:27 and 2:24 in asserting three particulars about God's actions in creation (follow Matt. 19:4–6 for Jesus' affirmation of three divine activities). First, God "made" them male and female (v. 4). Second, God "said" the creative design for marriage is for the male and female to leave their parents and be joined as one flesh (v. 5). Third, God "joined" them together in one flesh (CEB's "what God has put together"), which should not be undone by anyone (v. 6). Jesus thus affirms that heterosexual gender is divinely created, heterosexual marriage is a divine institution, and heterosexual fidelity is the divine intent. Same-sex practices are thus a break from all three of these God-given purposes.[5]

The truth is that both testaments are universally negative about same-sex practices. And the New Testament "offers no accounts of homosexual Christians, tells no stories of same-sex lovers, ventures

---

5. For this way of formulating the argument, see John R. W. Stott, *Same-Sex Partnerships? A Christian Perspective* (Grand Rapids, MI: Baker Book House, 1998), 36; and for a "kingdom perspective" limiting sexual relationships, see Ben Witherington, *The Rest of Life: Rest, Play, Eating, Studying, Sex from a Kingdom Perspective* (Grand Rapids, MI: W. B. Eerdmans Publishing Company, 2012), 135–53, esp. 138–39.

no metaphors that place a positive construal on homo-sexual relations."[6] The same could be said about the Old Testament as well, of course. But the point here is that we must step beyond the reductionistic game of pitting text against text in a hopeless shouting match. The appeal to Scripture is more about divine revelation, and the need to discern the full-bodied vision of life with God, including the task of moral theology for exploring the divine intention for creation of the sexes and divine ideal for marriage.[7] We lose the forest when we spend so much time arguing over the trees. In the light of divine revelation, running across and through all of Scripture, the testimony of the Bible is that God celebrates and blesses heterosexual love enjoyed within the confines of monogamous faithfulness. There is no such celebration or blessing of same-sex relationships. Quite the contrary, the Bible consistently warns against them.

Since we cannot explain away the biblical evidence, how then can we be so divided on this issue? The answer

---

6. Hays, *Moral Vision*, 395.

7. On this need to "switch from Scripture to revelation" in the current debate, see William J. Abraham, "The Church's Teaching on Sexuality: A Defense of The United Methodist Church's *Discipline* on Homosexuality," in *Staying the Course: Supporting the Church's Position on Homosexuality,* ed. Maxie D. Dunnam and H. Newton Maloney (Nashville, TN: Abingdon Press, 2003), 15–31, esp. 23–26.

is simpler than it may at first appear. It has little to do with the *interpretation* of these individual passages of the Bible. There have been attempts to interpret the facts of Scripture differently in order to find pro-homosexual themes in the Bible. None have won acceptance. No, the *interpretation* of Scripture on this issue is hardly open for debate. But our disagreement is over the question of *how* (or even *if*) the Bible's teachings on same-sex practices carry cross-cultural significance today. This is not *interpretation* of what the Bible says about same-sex practices, but a process we call *evaluation* of the canonical message of Scripture (also known as *appropriation*).[8]

As we saw in the last chapter, we United Methodists embrace a high view of Scripture, reading the individual texts of both Old and New Testaments as one sacred canon, which we take as "the primary source and criterion for Christian doctrine." But the higher one's view of Scripture, the more crucial the issue of interpretation, or more precisely, the issue of evaluation or relevance in interpretation.[9] John Wesley should be our guide here, as he states in the preface to his sermons that he desires

---

8. David R. Bauer and Robert A. Traina, *Inductive Bible Study: A Comprehensive Guide to the Practice of Hermeneutics* (Grand Rapids, MI: Baker Academic, 2011), 279–335.

9. A point made by Joel B. Green, "Reading the Bible as Wesleyans," *Wesleyan Theological Journal* 33, no. 2 (1998): 116–29, esp. 116.

always to provide "plain truth for plain people."[10] This simple reading strategy is clear elsewhere in Wesley as he urged readers always to look for Scripture's plain, literal, historical sense (*sensus literalis*) unless a metaphorical intention is also clear.[11]

Put simply (and plainly), several voices from different portions of Scripture speak unanimously and with unity of opinion on this issue. Their collective voices come from across the canon, in a great diversity of expressions and cultural contexts. The transcultural significance of the Bible's view of same-sex practices is difficult to miss. Even if we admit we aren't quite clear how to read certain individual texts (like the two legal prohibitions of Leviticus or the narrative about Sodom in Genesis 19), the message of the whole canon is nevertheless clear. A canonical dialogue is taking place, and the conversation partners are all in agreement.

---

10. John Wesley, "Preface [to Sermons on Several Occasions]," in *The Works of John Wesley,* ed. Thomas Jackson, 3rd ed., 14 vols. (London: Wesleyan Methodist Book Room, 1872; repr., Grand Rapids, MI: Baker Book House, 1978), vol. 5, 1–6, esp. 2, ¶3. Specific to Wesley's reading strategies, see his "Preface" to the *Explanatory Notes upon the New Testament* (vol. 14, 235–39) and "Preface" to the *Explanatory Notes upon the Old Testament* (vol. 14, 246–53).

11. For quotes and references, see conveniently Thomas C. Oden, *John Wesley's Teachings, Volume 1: God and Providence* (Grand Rapids, MI: Zondervan, 2012), 67.

To bring this point home, imagine with me a round-table conversation of six or eight people over coffee. It's an interesting conversation about ideas, not unlike hundreds of conversations we have all enjoyed. But now imagine these dialogue partners are all authors of different parts of the Bible. Moses is there; so are Jeremiah, Luke, John, and Paul, and a couple more you don't recognize.[12] They've covered fascinating topics, like the goodness of creation, sin and atonement, forgiveness, care for the poor, resurrection and eternal life, and many others. They speak with different accents (even different languages), and are sometimes surprised by the way others around the table explain things. On certain topics, like resurrection, eternal life, and incarnation, Luke, John, and Paul have a great advantage. Their Old Testament dialogue partners are surprised at times, but they appreciate hearing how their own ideas have been developed and brought to deeper formulations.

Now imagine the group turns to the question of women in culture and ministry. Moses and Jeremiah explain that women in Israelite culture were limited by the inherent patriarchal nature of their ancient Near Eastern context. But all the same, Israelite women were

---

12. I am not making any particular authorial claim by the use of "Moses," only making a point in the illustration. And the presence of a couple of strangers is because much of the biblical text (especially the Old Testament) is written anonymously.

afforded leadership positions at times (like prophetesses or military roles, though not priests or kings), all of which was countercultural, even revolutionary for its time. In contrast to their surroundings, women in their time had elevated roles in Israelite society. Then John and Paul speak up and explain that the coming of Messiah resulted in even more advances for women. John tells a story of Rabbi Jesus conversing with a woman by a well, and Paul explains that women were even allowed into worship with the men. Of course, there remained restrictions and limitations due to their Greco-Roman culture. But the dialogue partners all recognize and affirm a trajectory, a discernible upward direction in their conversation about the role of women in church and society. If you and I were allowed to speak up in this conversation, standing in the background, we might explain to the group around the table that the trajectory they defined made it possible for today's Christians to work toward a thoroughly egalitarian church and society, although we would be quick to admit we still have work to do. Everyone around the table would be pleased with this news.[13]

---

13. For a scholarly version of this conversation, see David L. Thompson, "Women, Men, Slaves and the Bible: Hermeneutical Inquiries," *Christian Scholar's Review* 25, no. 3 (1996): 326–49. Thompson explains how the "canonical dialogue" creates a "trajectory" that compels us as readers to accept the target anticipated in

Now, imagine next that the conversation turns to the question of same-sex practices. Moses starts the conversation (as usual), and explains that these practices were perceived in different ways by ethicists in his day. Some saw it as degrading for the passive partner, and therefore they had certain legal restrictions against it. Some of the religions around Moses provided male cult functionaries (prostitutes) as part of their religious practices, while others condemned it as at least anomalous behavior.[14] Then Moses explains that, in contrast to their surroundings, Israel considered same-sex practices as an affront to Yahweh's redeeming action in bringing them out of Egypt.[15] Same-sex practices were therefore associated with other inappropriate behavior common in Egypt and Canaan (Lev. 18:3), from which they had been delivered. Such practices were condemned and

---

Scripture and toward which the Scripture trajectory is headed. In this case full egalitarian relationships between men and women in the church. For discussion of such a trajectory more narrowly within the legal material of the Pentateuch as it relates to the role of women and slaves in Israelite society, see Bruce C. Birch, *Let Justice Roll Down: The Old Testament, Ethics, and Christian Life* (Louisville, KY: Westminster/John Knox Press, 1991), 160–61.

14. Richard M. Davidson, *Flame of Yahweh: Sexuality in the Old Testament* (Peabody, MA: Hendrickson Publishers, 2007), 134–42.

15. Leviticus 18:22 and 20:13 condemn only male homosexual behavior due to the patriarchal context, as all the other laws in these chapters attest. The author of the Holiness Code would have likely said the same about female same-sex practices.

prohibited as part of Israel's new covenant obligation as a life of holiness in the Promised Land (Lev. 18:4–5; 19:2; 20:26). To engage in these practices would make Israelites no better than the Egyptians behind them or the Canaanites before them in the land they are supposed to inhabit. Israel would lose the Promised Land because of these practices. At this, Jeremiah and the other strangers sitting at the table would simply nod their heads in agreement. Luke and John would voice agreement by sharing the Messiah's convictions about marriage, and Paul would speak about similar Greco-Roman practices. In other words, there would be no trajectory here. There is no surprise or fuller revelation beyond Moses and Jeremiah. On this topic, all the dialogue partners recognize, not an upward direction in the conversation, as we saw on the role of women, but a consistent agreement, more like a flatline consensus. Everyone around this table is in agreement.

By this simple illustration, you can see the powerful message of Scripture in one voice warning against same-sex practices. And yet it has been suggested recently that our current crisis is the result of reducing our two Testaments of Christian Scripture to phases in the history of religions.[16] Many in our church have reduced the Old

---

16. For more on this, see Christopher R. Seitz, *The Character of Christian Scripture: The Significance of a Two-Testament Bible* (Grand

Testament to a book that describes an earlier phase in the history of religion in a way that strips its status as canon for the church. In this way, it is assumed that the New Testament improves upon the Old, and that finally, we have arrived at a new religious phase in our day that improves upon them both, providing a new moral imperative for sexual behavior. The two Testaments have been relegated to the status of historical witnesses, which are somehow superseded by the superior wisdom of today's church. In this way, the hospitality argument really is vulnerable to the charge of failing to "take the Bible seriously."

The past forty years of debate over same-sex practices have seen three separate and distinct phases in the church's understanding of Scripture on this issue.[17] In phase one, biblical passages on same-sex practices were reevaluated. It was argued these texts had been misunderstood for centuries; no one has gotten them quite right until now. So, for example, the sin of the citizens of Sodom was taken as a violation of hospitality laws (Gen. 19:1–29). Paul in Romans 1:18–32, it was argued, is

---

Rapids, MI: Baker Academic, 2011), 190. Seitz is writing from his context in the Anglican Communion, which is quite parallel to the debate in the UMC.

17. These phases are detailed in Christopher R. Seitz, *Character of Christian Scripture*, 176–77. Again, Seitz is writing from his perspective in the Anglican Communion, but the issues are identical.

condemning exotic kinds of same-sex misconduct, not same-sex practices themselves. This phase was marked by confidence that we had finally gotten biblical studies right. We were correcting the misreadings of the past.

In phase two, however, these results were reversed. Most readers admitted, even those in favor of celebrating and endorsing same-sex practices, that the biblical texts say what previous generations of Christians believed they were saying. The Bible really is consistently negative toward same-sex practices, despite attempts to read it otherwise. A new strategy was needed. In this phase, it was argued that the Bible provides only a rough guide for how to make decisions. In fact, the Council of Jerusalem (Acts 15 and other stories, such as Acts 10–11) was said to illustrate how the early Christians made decisions about accepting and including Gentile Christians into what had otherwise been a Jewish movement until then. Acceptance and inclusion of gay Christians into today's church, it was argued, should be patterned after the paradigm of the early church, which expanded its horizons by recognizing God's Spirit at work in individuals previously excluded from the fellowship. Many have raised doubts about whether the analogy with first-century Gentile Christians is appropriate or pertinent enough to override all the other factors in the debate.[18]

---

18. For example, Richard B. Hays, *Moral Vision*, 396.

Finally, in phase three, where we currently find ourselves, some argue what the Bible teaches on same-sex practices is irrelevant. What some recognize today, it is argued, as monogamous faithful homosexuality was simply not known or understood in ancient times. We shouldn't expect the Bible to speak a word directly to us on this question because the issue of same-sex behavior lies developmentally beyond the range of its religious progression. In this phase, much emphasis may be placed on development change and progress (see the next chapter) and the role of the Holy Spirit in leading the church into a new understanding and appreciation of homosexual love. Parallel to these three phases is a reduction of Scripture to "a book of religious develop-ment, from one Testament to the next," and ultimately, to our enlightened modern times.[19]

In such an approach the Bible has lost all canonical authority. The plain sense of Scripture has been reduced to a resource for thinking about doctrine, but it has no real voice. It becomes a collection of quaint stories, maxims, and parables for reflection upon our present life-experiences. Instead, today's testimonies of individuals purposely embracing and celebrating same-sex practices are offered as evidence for changing the church's stance. We have replaced the authority of

19. Seitz, *Character of Christian Scripture*, 177.

Scripture with the authority of experience. And this in the name of progress, a topic we will revisit in the next chapter.

Humility or Boldness: Equal Virtues?

While in this neighborhood, I need to return to an earlier topic that I addressed only briefly: the role of humility in our current debate. The idea just explored—that today's church has a superior understanding of same-sex practices that should lead us to correct Scripture—requires me to return now to this question. Are we so enlightened today that we should overturn Scripture and tradition on the question of same-sex practices?

Remember that Adam Hamilton's book *Seeing Gray* presents a subtle shift away from truth-seeking as the primary objective in our current struggle as a church (see my summary in chapter 1). In a chapter entitled "Straining Gnats," he lumps together "our quest for truth," "certainty," and "purity of doctrine," with "our tendency to label others who don't agree with us, to separate from them and to demonize them."[20] On the next page, he states rather bluntly that "ultimately, what is needed is

---

20. Adam Hamilton, *Seeing Gray in a World of Black and White: Thoughts on Religion, Morality, and Politics* (Nashville, TN: Abingdon Press, 2008), 13.

humility," and adds that humility is essential to Christian faith.[21]

Of course, humility is vital to Christian faith, *by definition*. To admit that one is incapable of saving oneself, to admit that I am lost and need grace and forgiveness, is itself humbling. We all need a Savior. I have identified this line of reasoning as a distraction away from the real issue. It's an example of a *Red Herring Fallacy*, which introduces an idea into the discussion that is irrelevant to the issue at hand. The elevation of humility as our greatest need essentially changes the subject. Is it true that Christians today are arrogant? Sometimes. Does that mean they are mistaken on this or that social issue? Of course not.

There is a twofold irony in the call for more humility. First, it occurs to me that an approach that admits that Scripture is clear on same-sex practices, but at the same time, argues that "we know better today" is itself vulnerable to a charge of having too little humility. Folks on either side of the debate can be full of pride or marked by humility. We all need more humility. Yes! But if I disagree with you, it doesn't mean I do so because I have too much pride.

Second, the call for more humility in our debate is ironic because the Israelites, after the exodus, the

---

21. Hamilton, *Seeing Gray*, 14.

wilderness covenant, the conquest of the Promised Land, and other blessings of life with God, were gifted with a certain bold confidence (exemplified in Josh. 1:5–6). Similarly, the first Christians were certainly called upon to muster up courage in abundance, in equal amounts to their humility. And church leaders in the first three centuries of Christianity had leaders known more for bold and frank courage than for humility as such. You get the picture. Humility is important. No one disagrees. But so are boldness and courage in standing for what one believes to be true and right. Which virtue is greater?

Of course, the answer is that Christians need both confidence and humility. But allow me to draw you further into this topic by calling upon the inimitable G. K. Chesterton to remind us how seriously mistaken is this call for humility, as though this is our ultimate need. Chesterton's book *Orthodoxy* includes a chapter entitled "The Suicide of Thought."[22] He is concerned that numerous vices have been let loose in the world to wander aimlessly in the hearts of humans, where they do great damage. But the world is also far too good, filled with wild and wasted virtues, which also wander aimlessly and which result in more damage still. The

---

22. For more on this, and for all quotes from Chesterton in this discussion, see G. K. Chesterton, *Orthodoxy* (New York and London: John Lane, 1909), 52–80.

problem is that Christian virtues have been isolated from each other, striped of their theological moorings in Christianity, and wander alone.

After briefly mentioning truth-seeking, compassion, and charity, Chesterton goes on to discuss "the remarkable case of the dislocation of humility." He describes humility as the primary way to confine our arrogance and limit the otherwise unlimited appetite of humanity. It is Christian humility, says Chesterton, that makes other virtues possible, such as pleasure and joy. The next part of his discussion is so instructive that I have included it here slightly revised (excusing his 1909 gender-exclusive language).

> [W]hat we suffer from today is humility in the wrong place. Modesty has moved from the organ of ambition. Modesty has settled upon the organ of conviction; where it was never meant to be. A man was meant to be doubtful about himself, but undoubting about the truth; this has been exactly reversed. Nowadays the part of a man that a man does assert is exactly the part he ought not to assert—himself. The part he doubts is exactly the part he ought not to doubt—the Divine Reason. [Biologist Thomas Henry] Huxley preached a humility content to learn from Nature. But the new skeptic is so humble that he doubts if he can even learn. Thus we should be wrong if we had said hastily

that there is no humility typical of our time. The truth is that there is a real humility typical of our time; but it so happens that it is practically a more poisonous humility than the wildest prostrations of the ascetic.[23]

Chesterton makes the point that humility has a proper location; it rightly belongs with us, to check and counterbalance our natural human drives and ambitions. That is true Christian humility. We ought always to remember that we humans are grasping and greedy individuals whenever left unattended by the restraining features of God's grace. And this is humbling, to be sure. But that humility has been misplaced in our time (a full century after it was first observed by Chesterton to be so). Whereas it belongs naturally with us, our humility has left us and rested instead upon "the truth" or "Divine Reason." While humility rests there rather than upon us, our now unattended grasping natures raise doubts about whether any of us can know anything really. Do any of us have any right to search for truth, or claim to have confidence in the absolute certainty of anything? As Adam Hamilton puts it, "the hope for the future of Christianity will be found, in part, in our willingness to accept that no one of us has all of the truth."[24]

---

23. Chesterton, *Orthodoxy*, 55.
24. Hamilton, *Seeing Gray*, 13.

Of course, on one level this last quote from Adam is another red herring (irrelevant distraction) because no one is claiming to have "all of the truth." But what is the implication? Am I immodest or lacking in humility if I express confidence in having *some* truth? What about *lots* of truth? *How much* truth can I claim without sounding full of pride? Building on Chesterton's point, I contend that we can and should proclaim with plenty of immodest pride that we have the truth of the gospel. And we should proclaim the truth of that gospel with courage, boldness, and confidence. And we should also proclaim it with humility that, no, we don't have "all of the truth." But like Wesley, we can declare with confidence: "God himself has condescended to teach the way: for this very end he came from heaven. He hath written it down in a book. O give me that book! At any price, give me the book of God! I have it: Here is knowledge enough for me."[25]

In sum, it is an unfair distraction to suggest that humility will bring us closer together on human sexuality. Those who favor retaining our church's stance against same-sex practices are driven by tenacity and urgency.[26] They are *tenacious* because they believe the position they hold rests firmly on Scripture, reason, tradition, and

---

25. Wesley, "Preface [to Sermons on Several Occasions]," 3, ¶5.
26. Abraham, "Church's Teaching on Sexuality," 28–29.

experience, and to relinquish that position would be tantamount to walking away from the gospel message of grace and forgiveness. They are *urgent* because they believe the pressure to change the church's stance against same-sex practices is undermining the church's mission, and threatens to cripple Methodism permanently. Are some full of pride and conceit? Perhaps. Does that make them wrong? Certainly not.

Wesley's "Catholic Spirit"

Is it time for the UMC to chart new territory? If we are truly standing at a fork in the road, admitting that Scripture divides us into two options—holiness or hospitality—perhaps the prophetic ministry of our church must lead us to forge ahead in a new direction. Assuming a third way can be found on same-sex practices, is it necessarily to be preferred?

We Methodists love to quote Wesley's sermon on the "Catholic Spirit" in these debates. So let's turn to it for insight on whether the quest for a third-way solution to our current debate is preferable. Typically, the sermon is used to appeal for unity above all else: *If your heart is as my heart, then give me your hand.*[27] What a beautiful

---

27. Only an approximate quote from the sermon (¶II.2). The sermon draws on the KJV translation of 2 Kings 10:15: "Is thine heart

sentiment. The sermon is Wesley's appeal for Christian love especially when Christians differ, and its use in our church today illustrates the degree to which we have elevated unity as an ultimate virtue. Indeed, sometimes The United Methodist Church values unity and inclusion above all else.

Wesley begins by acknowledging that Christians "can't all think alike" and because of this, "they can't all walk alike." These two general hindrances mean that Christians will have differences in practice because they have differences of conviction. Unity of opinion is not always possible, but unity of love is. Though we cannot all think alike, we may certainly love alike; we are not of one mind, but we can be of one heart.

> And 'tis certain, so long as "we know" but "in part," that all men will not see all things alike. It is an unavoidable consequence of the present weakness and shortness of human understanding that several men will be of several minds, in religion as well as in common life. So it has been from the beginning

---

right, as my heart is with thy heart? And Jehonadab answered, It is. If it be, give me thine hand. And he gave him his hand; and he took him up to him into the chariot." The relevance of Jehu's quote is beyond the scope of my point here. All quotes of the sermon in this section are from "Catholic Spirit," *The Sermons of John Wesley: A Collection for the Christian Journey,* ed. Kenneth J. Collins and Jason E. Vickers (Nashville, TN: Abingdon Press, 2013), 420–30.

of the world, and so it will be "till the restitution of all things."

Wesley continues by asserting that all of us have convictions and opinions we hold to be true. And yet all of us understand that we cannot be correct in every respect and on every issue. Indeed, we can all be confident that every one of us is incorrect on some issues. We simply don't know in what particulars we are mistaken. And since all of us are alike in this way, we must surely grant allowances to each other as fellow Christians to live with our differing opinions. "Every wise man therefore will allow others the same liberty of thinking which he desires they should allow him; and will no more insist on their embracing his opinions than he would have them to insist on his embracing theirs."[28]

Christians therefore understand that each of us is called to follow the dictates of conscience "in simplicity and godly sincerity." Acting upon the "best light" available to us, we must all allow differences of opinion on forms of worship, of church government, forms of prayer, and forms of the administration of the sacraments of Communion and baptism. We can and should agree to

---

28. Note that Wesley is focused in this sermon on differing opinions on forms and modes of worship, which may be more instructive for today's "worship wars" than for our debate on same-sex practices.

disagree on such features of Christian worship and practice among various Christian denominations.

Wesley then explores our common convictions that are essentials in our Christian faith. These are the convictions that determine whether our hearts are alike: our understanding of the nature of God, of Jesus Christ and him crucified, the indwelling presence of the Spirit of Christ transforming our lives, and whether we are in love with God (heart, mind, soul, and strength). Are we contented in God and employed in the work of God? Are we singularly focused on pleasing God above all others? Are we in love and charity with our neighbors, loving and praying for blessings for those who despise and abuse us? If we are so minded, then yes, Wesley says, our hearts are alike, and we can agree to disagree on forms of worship.

If we are in agreement on these essentials, we join hands as fellow Christians. We need not expect or even desire to change each other's minds on specific forms of worship or the meaning of the sacraments. I'll keep my opinions; you keep yours. Honestly, we can't help ourselves. I have no ability simply to change my mind on these matters of conviction, nor should I expect you to change your mind. Specifically, Wesley refers to an episcopal form of church government as the one he believes is scriptural and apostolic. Yet he will embrace as a fellow Christian anyone who, for reasons of conscience, prefers non-episcopal forms. He believes infant baptism is scriptural. He believes that formal, written prayers are as acceptable in public worship as extemporaneous prayers. Beyond these, as fellow Christians, we ought to love each other, pray for each other, and encourage each other to do good works in the name of Christ.

In the last portion of the sermon, Wesley turns to the question "what is a 'catholic spirit'?" by which he means an all-embracing spirit—a Christian of the catholic ("universal") church. He defines the catholic spirit initially by listing three things it is not. First, a catholic spirit "is not speculative latitudinarianism." A Christian with a catholic spirit is not indifferent to all opinions, but is rather "fixed as the sun in his judgment concerning the main branches of Christian doctrine." Such a one is not of a "muddy understanding," or lacking in any "settled, consistent principles," and is not in favor of "jumbling all opinions together."

Second, a catholic spirit "is not any kind of practical latitudinarianism." Here Wesley applies what he has said to the question of various forms of worship. While we are to love each other, pray, and encourage each other in Christ, we accept our differences relative to forms and expressions of worship, even on the nature and practice of the sacraments. But we are not indifferent about public worship. We hold our opinions because we have searched Scripture and searched other forms of worship everywhere in the world, and therefore have "no doubt, no scruple at all" about our own convictions on the proper form of worship.

Third, a catholic spirit is not indifferent to "all congregations," by which Wesley means this Christian of a catholic spirit is committed to a single communion of believers. The catholic spirit "is fixed in his congregation," and regularly partakes in the worship of God. Having described what the catholic spirit is not, Wesley concludes such a Christian is characterized by "catholic or universal love."

The sermon offers help for followers of Wesley on the question of ecumenical love and cooperation among Christians who differ on non-essential practices of worship. The specific issues he addresses have to do with the forms of worship, and the nature and administration of the sacraments. This brief survey is enough to give us pause about the way the sermon is so frequently quoted, especially the phrase, *If your heart is as my heart, then give me your hand.* Wesley's sermon emphasizes ecumenical love and cooperation among denominations that have strongly held convictions that simply cannot be overcome.

Yet Wesley's resounding statements about latitudinarianism are just as instructive. Here we have a warning against the vagaries of broadmindedness, or uncritical tolerance, or any sort of indifference about exploratory theology (his "speculative latitudinarianism") or indifference regarding worship or the administration of the sacraments ("practical latitudinarianism"). Wesley is certainly not advocating a laissez-faire or tolerant approach to Christian doctrine, as though unity in belief and doctrine is irrelevant as long as we have unity in mission and social justice. The often quoted line from the sermon—*Though we can't think alike, may we not love alike?*—is most often *mis*quoted to represent a Wesleyan "think and let think" ideology. All of this needs to be held in balance with Wesley's forceful and unambiguous attacks on the Deism and Arianism (and other low Christologies) of his day, and to a lesser extent, even his criticisms of Roman Catholicism ("Papists" as opposed to Eastern Orthodoxy).[29]

Ironically, this sermon admonishes us in the Wesleyan tradition to stand firm on doctrines and principles we believe to be rooted in Scripture and reason. The Old Testament text in view—"Are you as committed to me as I am to you?" (2 Kings 10:15)—has little to do with one's heart as the seat of emotions, but more with one's opinions and convictions.[30] Wesley understands this

---

29. Kenneth J. Collins, *The Theology of John Wesley: Holy Love and the Shape of Grace* (Nashville, TN: Abingdon Press, 2007), 89.

30. H. J. Fabry, "Heart" in *Theological Dictionary of the Old Testament,* ed. G. J. Botterweck, H. Ringgren, and H. J. Fabry, trans.

perfectly, as is clear from the beginning of the sermon when he refers to differences of "opinions or modes of worship" preventing full unity among Christians. The text and sermon start with theological convictions, and not the feelings and affections of our hearts. It isn't true that you and I should simply overlook our differences if we really like each other.

"Catholic Spirit" as a sermon casts a beautiful vision of love and fellowship with other Christian communions. We may disagree with other believers on matters important to us, such as worship and the sacraments. Yet Wesley is not talking about essential matters of orthodox doctrine. Rather, as fellow Christians, we need not focus on those differences but love, pray for, and encourage each other. However, the sermon certainly does not blithely encourage unity within the United Methodist fellowship at the expense of a high Christology, an atonement theory deeply rooted in the metaphors of Scripture, a robust ecclesiology grounded in the early church, or a number of other theological issues. Nor does Wesley's

---

J. T. Willis, G. W. Bromiley, and D. E. Green, 8 vols. (Grand Rapids, MI: W. B. Eerdmans Publishing Company), vol. 7, 399–437, esp. 419–21 on the heart as the noetic center of cognition. The CEB is somewhat misleading here. Jehu's question is literally, "*Is your heart upright*, as my heart is with your heart?" (my translation). The sentiment is not simply, "If your heart is as my heart . . ." The question begins "Is your heart right . . ." If so, and my heart is as your heart, then . . .

sermon elevate unity as a first-degree virtue in our own communion. The use of the phrase, *If your heart is as my heart* as a call to keep united in United Methodism above all else is indefensible. It's a misquoting of Wesley to use "think, and let think" (or, "agree to disagree") within our own communion as a call to change the church's stance on same-sex practices.

Compromise or Compromise?

So we return now to the question. If a middle-way solution between holiness and hospitality were *possible*, would it necessarily be *preferable*? Would a tertium quid be genuine compromise in the best sense of that word—a healthy settlement in which both sides make some concession? Or, would it merely be a compromise in the very worst sense of that word—a surrendering of principle?

It is reasonable to say that no one of us, on either side of the debate, wants the other to surrender ideals or principles. Neither should any one of us make compromises because it makes us feel more humble, or simply because we want to avoid the charge of being prideful. Nor do the virtues of unity and inclusion settle the issue. We hold both of these virtues in high esteem in United Methodism. But more than these, we seek to settle our debate primarily on the basis of Scripture, confirmed by reason, illumined by tradition, and brought to life in experience.

Helmut Thielicke has encouraged the church of every generation to understand itself as engaged in a continuous debate between the gospel and the self-understanding of the age, between "eternity and time."[31] This is true, he asserts, because Christian faith believes *against* as well as *in*; that is, faith self-consciously runs counter to the currents in modern ideological stream. Christian theology has a polar structure; one pole is "a superior, eternal basis derived from revelation," while the other is "specific constellations of the spirit of the age within and against which it makes its statements."

Given the clarity of Scripture's renunciation of same-sex practices, United Methodism's overreaching commitments to misplaced humility and unity have created a crisis of theological reasoning in the church. Compromise appears neither possible nor preferable.

---

31. Helmut Thielicke, *Modern Faith and Thought*, trans. Geoffrey W. Bromiley (Grand Rapids, MI: W. B. Eerdmans Publishing Company, 1990), 5–7.

5

A Funny Thing Happened on the Way to Utopia

If we learned anything from the twentieth century, it is this: progress is not inevitable. Change is inevitable, yes. But this is not the same as progress. The last century was defined by two world wars separated by a global economic depression, followed in the second half of the century by a so-called cold war that saw millions oppressed or murdered by totalitarian regimes. The cheery optimism of the nineteenth century was crushed by events of the twentieth century.

In this book, I began by questioning Adam Hamilton's third-way approach as it relates to The United Methodist Church's debate over same-sex practices. Along the way,

I have objected that his book *Seeing Gray* especially accepts an unwarranted assumption (that is, it begs a question) about whether or not such a third-way approach is possible. In the previous chapter, we explored another unwarranted assumption—whether such an approach is preferable. Here, I want to offer a continuation of that thought by suggesting another way Adam is question begging by assuming such a middle-road solution (were it possible) would necessarily be *progress*. By presenting the issues in this way, I will demonstrate that Adam's proposals do not mean progress for the church, or (in the next chapter) for individuals who experience same-sex attraction.

Once again, remember that begging the question is a logical fallacy that involves unwarranted assumptions. The question in this chapter is whether a middle-way solution on same-sex practices, if one could be found, would necessarily mean progress for the church, and most especially in our context, The United Methodist Church. Those on the hospitality side of the debate, who want to change the UMC's stance against same-sex practices, often assume such a change would be progress. Is it true? Would changing our opposition on this issue be progress? Or would it, in fact, be the opposite?

At the root of this fallacy is the idea that progress is inevitable. Eventually, it is believed, given enough time and cooperation among humans across the planet, society will move toward greater and better, or more advanced stages resulting in a better life for all. The only deterrents are individuals, institutions, and systems stuck in doing things the way they've always been done, the old ways that are hurtful to human progress, ways that unfortunately slow down the rate of progress.

Many people today subconsciously associate this to the way we relate in our rapidly changing world to science and technology. Just as we use faster and more powerful computers every day, or as we understand our ever-expanding universe more profoundly, or as our ability to cure diseases increases, so humanity in general will slowly evolve to higher and better stages of advancement. Some skeptics and agnostics believe religion itself will no longer be necessary because humanity will simply outgrow the need for what they consider to be superstitious rituals that are dangerous, simplistic, irrational, and outdated.[1] In other cases, Christians assume faith itself is part of an evolutionary progress, as much as science and technology. In this way, Christian faith and doctrine need constant reforming and transforming.

---

1. A growing secularist culture is taking shape in the West, often linked to this optimistic view that things will improve over time, especially if the toxic effects of religion can be minimized. Jacques Berlinerblau, *The Secular Bible: Why Nonbelievers Must Take Religion Seriously* (Cambridge and New York: Cambridge University Press, 2005).

Is any of this true? Is it partly true? In order to get to the heart of the way this assumption of progress relates to our current debates in the UMC, we now turn to an important question you must answer.

Are You Liberal or Conservative?[2]

Seeing Gray proposes a third way for the UMC between the left and the right, or liberals and conservatives, where they can meet at the "radical center."[3] However, when one drills down to the specifics of what he longs for as a radical center, one finds a familiar friend, someone who has been offering alternatives for a long while. The core doctrinal commitments of Wesleyan theology have been offering a balanced worldview for two centuries, hammered out on a black-and-white anvil of critical theological reasoning. I concluded in chapter 2 that much of what Adam is proposing as a new radical core is really only where Wesleyan theology has been for many years.

At the same time, I find much of Adam's discussion of what he calls the "theological divide" to be helpful, and this will be a useful starting point for our discussion. Adam

---

2. Borrowed from Adam Hamilton's first chapter title.

3. Adam Hamilton, *Seeing Gray in a World of Black and White: Thoughts on Religion, Morality, and Politics* (Nashville, TN: Abingdon Press, 2008), 232.

rightly identifies the problems in these labels "liberal" and "conservative."[4] He explains that he attended a somewhat conservative college (Oral Roberts University) and then a somewhat liberal seminary (Perkins School of Theology at Southern Methodist University). Thanks to this diverse education, Adam says he was able to explore "the truth found on both sides of the theological divide."[5] And thus he argues the labels we so often use are inadequate. Many Christians today, he claims, are unwilling to identify with either conservative or liberal, and he offers his tertium quid (or, middle-way) as an alternative way of thinking, one that he hopes will reform Christianity.

I agree with Adam that the labels "liberal" and "conservative," or "traditionalist" and "progressive," or any number of other labels, are inadequate. None are very helpful in summarizing all the commitments of each side over and against the other in a theological debate. And any of these quickly become pejorative and hurtful when used against the other side in the heat of debate.[6]

---

4. Hamilton, *Seeing Gray,* 3–8.

5. Ibid., 4.

6. One prominent scholar attempted to alleviate the problem by using *conservatives* for those who want to conserve the current Methodist position, and *revisionists* for those who want to revise the present position. When that didn't work, he referred to *conservative* and *liberal*, and denied that anything like a *centrist* view has been possible. William J. Abraham, "The Church's Teaching on Sexuality: A Defense of The United Methodist Church's *Discipline*

The inadequacy of the labels is easily demonstrated by two examples Adam shares.[7] One friend is a liberal pastor who opposes abortion but favors allowing same-sex marriage-like covenants. Another pastor friend is conservative but is focused on the environment and poverty, and favors raising taxes to address these concerns.

To these examples, I add one rather famous case to illustrate again the inadequacy of the easy use of these labels. United Methodist minister Maxie D. Dunnam is one of the most vocal advocates for maintaining the church's current position against same-sex practices. Few would dispute the assertion that Dr. Dunnam is one of the most conservative voices in the debate today.[8] But in 1963, when he was a young pastor in the Mississippi Conference of the UMC, he was one of four authors and original signers of a document titled "Born of Conviction," which was signed by twenty-eight ministers

---

on Homosexuality," in *Staying the Course: Supporting the Church's Position on Homosexuality*, ed. Maxie D. Dunnam and H. Newton Maloney (Nashville, TN: Abingdon Press, 2003), 188n9.

7. Hamilton, *Seeing Gray*, 5.

8. I have consulted his coedited book on this topic more than once: Maxie D. Dunnam and H. Newton Malony, eds., *Staying the Course: Supporting the Church's Position on Homosexuality* (Nashville, TN: Abingdon Press, 2003).

of the conference.[9] The document, written and signed a little more than three months after James Meredith became the first African-American student enrolled at the segregated University of Mississippi, caused quite a firestorm across the South. The document voiced opposition to racial segregation and called for desegregation of all public schools. Dr. Dunnam and the signers of the document were considered extremists, upstart "neophite [sic] preacher resolutors" and in the political climate of 1963, they were accused of being communists.[10] In that time and place, Dr. Dunnam's conservative theology led him to take a position that some considered liberal.

As Adam Hamilton says, "liberal and conservative are relative terms." On this we can agree. He goes further, however, to suggest that we should consider "both liberal and conservative as two parts of a whole" and that the inadequacies of these labels show "the world is not always black and white." He wants us to seek the

---

9. Joseph T. Reiff, "Conflicting Convictions in White Mississippi Methodism: The 1963 'Born of Conviction' Controversy," *Methodist History* 49, no. 3 (2011): 162–78; idem, "Born of Conviction: White Methodist Witness to Mississippi's Closed Society," in *Courage to Bear Witness: Essays in Honor of Gene L. Davenport,* ed. L. Edward Phillips and Billy Vaughan (Eugene, OR: Pickwick Publications, 2009), 124–42.

10. For the "resolutors" quote, see Joseph T. Reiff, "Conflicting Convictions," 164.

gray between them.[11] As with Adam's overall approach, he begs the question whether such a synthesis of liberal and conservative is possible. Here I want to ask more directly whether it would mean progress.

Let us clarify first what is usually meant by these labels, inadequate as they are.

Conservative. In the broadest possible categories, a theological conservative may be said to focus on preserving the kernel of divine revelation inspired in Scripture and handed down through the centuries to our day. You might think of conservatives as Christians who believe their faith is anchored in an idealized past, in which God's people were redeemed through the mighty acts of God. They are most conscious of "Keep this festival" types of commands in Scripture, calling upon believers to commemorate for all time what God has done in the mighty acts of salvation in the past: "Remember this day . . ." at the institution of Passover for the Israelites (Exod. 13:3), and "Do this in remembrance of me" at the institution of the Lord's Supper (Luke 22:19; 1 Cor. 5:8). Most conservatives believe the truth of the gospel was revealed in the Scripture and crystallized in the ecumenical councils of the church, especially the first four councils (Nicaea, Constantinople, Ephesus,

---

11. For all quotations in this paragraph, see Hamilton, *Seeing Gray*, 5–8.

and Chalcedon) during the first five centuries of church history. Conservatives are committed to passing on the revealed truth of the gospel and the church to the next generation of believers.

Conservatives tend to see truth as absolute. It is not evolving or changing, but abstract and revealed. They share a certain calling to "fight for the faith delivered once and for all to God's holy people" as a deposit of apostolic faith (Jude 3). They also tend to be somewhat pessimistic about the future. Their eschatology (doctrine of end times) expects nothing essentially positive or final until God dramatically intervenes to restore the kingdom of God as it originally was but has been lost in a fallen world. Finally, we should add a word about what conservatives are not. They are not obscurantists or reactionaries who have their heads in the sand. They are not afraid of change.

Liberal. In similarly broad categories, a theological liberal may be said to focus on expanding the kernel of divine revelation inspired in Scripture and handed down through the centuries to our day. You might think of liberals as Christians who believe their faith is anchored in an idealized community, a body of redeemed believers on a journey together. They are most conscious of Jesus' words to the first Christians: "I have much more to say to you, but you can't handle it now. However, when the Spirit of Truth comes, he will guide you in all truth"

(John 16:12–13). They are committed to following the Spirit of Truth into new insights of the gospel for the sake of the next generation of believers. At critical turning points in church history, it is believed, the Holy Spirit leads the church in updating and revising the faith in order to make it truer to the gospel and more relevant for contemporary settings. Some liberals believe it is idolatrous to entomb the truth of the gospel in abstract orthodoxy, as though it can be reduced to fixed expressions of doctrinaire ideologies.

Liberals often see truth as relative. It is certainly anchored in the past of God's revelation in Scripture, and in that sense is absolute. But truth paradoxically points to new insight under the inspiration of the Spirit of Truth as discerned by the church. Such new truth is always met with resistance because Christians are too often embedded in cultural restraints (patriarchy, sexism, racism, etc.), making it difficult to follow God into new understandings. Liberals also tend to be optimistic about the future. Their eschatology believes the church, with God's help, is in the process of ushering in the kingdom of God. Liberals are not anti-Scripture reformers who campaign and advocate for change just for the sake of change.

Of course, it is patently absurd to reduce all Christians to these two (and only two) ways of seeing the world and understanding our faith. Such brief descriptions as these are almost offensive, and I'm quite certain that liberals and conservatives will both take offense at what I have written, crying that this is a gross oversimplification. And so it is! But this is enough to make my point.

Essentially, the difference between liberals and conservatives is where they locate utopia—defined here as the kingdom of God with all its salutary benefits for citizens of that kingdom. Most conservatives think of God's perfect community as having been given at the beginning of time (Gen. 1–2) and in the early church (book of Acts). The goal of Christians is to make today's church and society as close to that ancient ideal as possible, with God's help. Liberals tend to think of the coming kingdom of God as the fuller expression of God's community. The ancient ideal was just a beginning, beyond which God is leading the church into ever-expanding understandings and fulfillments of God's grace. For the conservative, sin has a specific definition and is what ruined God's utopian past. For the liberal, sin is anything that prevents us from building the kingdom of God today.

Now my point is a simple one. These are both deeply rooted worldview configurations. They are intrinsic patterns of thinking about the world and about theology. Yet the labels "liberal" and "conservative" represent something even more innate. They are also deeply held convictions. It is overly simplistic and reductionistic to suggest they represent black-and-white alternatives, which must be overcome, or which *can* be overcome.

We shouldn't try to combine the best of both liberal and conservative ideologies in order to meet in the middle because they represent opposite ends of an ideological spectrum. They cannot both be right on this issue or the other. At times, they cannot be combined or merged. And in most cases, the spectrum includes a great many options between them.

With these observations, we have now returned to my main criticisms of Adam Hamilton's third-way approach. We simply cannot beg the question of whether a compromise is possible between liberals and conservatives. At times we have to admit we stand at a fork in the road dividing two positions. There is simply nothing we can do about that.

Furthermore, most of us would admit that on any issue about which we disagree, one position is right and another is wrong. One is true, the other false. That's simply the nature of disagreement or debate. At times compromises are possible, or tertium quid (middle-way) solutions can be found. But there are other times when these solutions are not possible. We simply must not beg the question of whether such a merger of two positions is something we *should* do. To deny these truth-claims on one side or the other is to fall into a hopeless fog of irrational speculation, epitomized by one form of postmodernism that thinks we can all be right. This is a logical cul-de-sac, as characterized succinctly by Harry G. Frankfurt.

[E]ven those who profess to deny the validity or the objective reality of the true-false distinction continue to maintain without apparent embarrassment that this denial is a position that they do *truly* endorse. The statement that they reject the distinction between true and false is, they insist, an unqualifiedly *true* statement about their beliefs, *not a false* one.[12]

I agree that *liberal* and *conservative* are inadequate terms because they reduce grand worldview configurations to convenient one-term labels that quickly become handles for insulting each other. On the other hand, these worldview configurations are real and simply cannot be merged, combing the best of both ends of the spectrum, in order to create a third-way solution. In theological terms, God's utopian ideal has both a primeval origin (*Urzeit*) and a final manifestation (*Endzeit*). But Christians have these opposing views of the church's role in bringing the kingdom of God to reality. Something has happened on the way to utopia.[13]

---

12. Harry G. Frankfurt, *On Truth* (New York: Knopf, 2006), 8–9.

13. The myth of progress is rooted in the Enlightenment's optimism and marked by its hope of a utopian future, which was a secularization and debasement of genuine Christian hope. Such progressivism sets aside transcendence, since it no longer depends on the actions of God in the world, but turns instead to the "immanent possibilities of the historical process itself." Richard Bauckham, "Emerging Issues in Eschatology in the Twenty-First Century," in *The*

The Image of Utopia

Earlier I took up seven topics that Adam Hamilton discusses in *Seeing Gray* in order to test the claim that he offers a middle way forward for Christianity. These were mostly theological issues that Christians often debate, and which Adam included in a section he called "The Bible, Beliefs, and the Spiritual Journey." We saw that in many of the disputed issues, Adam failed to recognize the roomy middle with other options already available. In many cases, perfectly good answers were already provided by Wesleyan forebears in our theological tradition.

Now we turn to the final issues Adam covers in a section entitled "Politics and Ethics in the Center."

1. Ethics

One controversy dividing liberals and conservatives, according to Adam Hamilton, is Christian ethics.[14] He begins with a summary of so-called situation ethics and then turns to an attempt to find middle ground between conservatives and liberals on this issue, by which he

---

Oxford Handbook of Eschatology, ed. Jerry L. Walls (Oxford and New York: Oxford University Press, 2008), 671–89, esp. 673–78. This secularizing myth of progress is taken up again in the next chapter as the "myth of liberation."

14. Hamilton, *Seeing Gray,* 147–52.

means a middle way between legalism (rules-based ethics) and libertinism (unrestrained ethics). The essential question is: How do you decide what is right and wrong?

In this discussion, Adam identifies Scripture, tradition, the church community (Wesley's "Christian conferencing"), and reason, essentially the Methodist quadrilateral, as "resources to help us live lives that would please God."[15] In the end, he rightly concludes situation ethics is inadequate because it relies solely on love of neighbor as a guiding principle. Instead, Christians are driven by love of God as a moral absolute, which ranks first in our priority for making moral decisions. In one important paragraph, Adam summarizes what he believes should be our guiding principles for moral decisions.

> There are a host of things I seek to avoid in life not because participating in them would harm anyone else, but because I don't believe they would honor and please God. There are courses of action I take in my life with an eye toward honoring God and expressing my love and devotion to him, though they have no direct bearing, good or bad, on another human being.[16]

---

15. Hamilton, *Seeing Gray*, 150.
16. Ibid., 151.

I agree completely with this assessment. Interestingly, I also believe Adam's assessment of Christian ethics and his principles for making moral decisions apply to our current debate over same-sex practices.

What is unclear to me is how this is "middle ground between conservatism and liberalism."[17] Presumably Adam sees love of God and neighbor as a compromise between legalistic conservatism and libertinistic liberalism. But to make such an assertion, one must also presume the very worst of both conservatives and liberals. Both could find cause for offense in his assumption (for example, that conservatives are legalists and liberals are lawless). In reality, this is not a middle-way, and offers no new path for twenty-first-century Christianity. This is simply Christian ethics, whether viewed from the left or the right (that is, liberals or conservatives).[18]

2. Abortion

Next we come to abortion, that intractable debate of our culture wars.[19] Adam assumes at the beginning that we will likely never find agreement on this issue

---

17. Ibid., 148.

18. On putting God first, see Christopher J. H. Wright, *Old Testament Ethics for the People of God* (Downers Grove, IL: Inter-Varsity Press, 2004), 23–47.

19. Hamilton, *Seeing Gray,* 153–63.

in the American debate. Nevertheless, he devotes this chapter to finding middle ground between the polarized extremes, even though he admits many positions in the middle presently exist.

Adam rightly struggles to find a middle way on this issue. For obvious *biological* reasons, a middle-way solution is harder to find. After fairly considering the concerns of both sides, he proposes a number of ways the two might meet in the middle. First, he suggests both sides should be able to accept the preference of birth control over abortion. Second, he proposes that we as a society "reclaim the sense of the sacredness of sex among young people" by encouraging abstinence. He proposes that liberals and conservatives could unite to produce serious advertising campaigns, enlisting Hollywood to help, in an effort to change attitudes of the young, teaching them that sex is something beautiful and holy, which binds two people together in profound ways, as opposed to something everyone does after a couple of dates. He bemoans our culture's glorification of casual or recreational sex. Both sides could surely work to reduce unwanted pregnancies, and lead the church to support women who choose to carry the child to term rather than have an abortion.

Adam favors the use of the morning-after pill as an alternative to surgical abortions. At the same time, he warns about the number of repeat abortions, indicating that for some, abortion is a means of birth control. He regrets that the life of a "developing human being is not taken seriously enough" in our culture.

Then Adam concludes the chapter with a beautiful illustration. He shares a personal and intimate letter from a woman who chose not to have an abortion when she was an unwed seventeen-year-old. Against the insistence of her father, she moved away from home, married her sixteen-year-old boyfriend, and lived with his family. They both dropped out of high school, and struggled to care for the newborn son. Unfortunately, twelve years later, the marriage ended in divorce. The woman then testifies that, although the pregnancy changed her life, her son became "the greatest blessing to me and thousands of others." She explains in the letter that she could not follow her father's advice and abort her baby. She had learned in Sunday school classes as a child to see the pregnancy as "a gift from God." Then, in a surprise ending, we learn that the woman who wrote the letter is Adam Hamilton's mother. He is the child she refused to abort.

The chapter closes with the reality that as much as 75 percent of the one million abortions in the United States each year are unrelated to concerns for the health of the mother, the health of the baby, rape, or incest. He calls for both sides to work together to end unwanted pregnancies.

In some ways, Adam has presented here a strong pro-life position, especially the personal illustration that he himself was an "accident." Although I appreciate his efforts to find a middle ground between the polarized positions on abortion, the truth is Adam has essentially presented our official United Methodist position on this question. Our Social Principles affirm our "belief in the sanctity of unborn human life," making us "reluctant to approve abortion."[20] While admitting the complexity of cases in which the life of either the mother or the baby is at risk, we recognize some such cases in which legal abortion should be an option. We unequivocally reject abortion as a means of birth control or gender selection. We also oppose late-term abortions. The United Methodist Church also calls for careful attention to be given to the conditions that lead to unwanted pregnancies, and commits the church to working to diminish the current high rate of abortions. We also encourage adoption as an alternative to abortion. In sum, much of what Adam proposes here is beautifully affirmed by our United Methodist Social Principles, and I agree with him that it offers the world a generally balanced way of thinking about this difficult issue.

---

20. *The Book of Discipline of The United Methodist Church 2012* (Nashville, TN: The United Methodist Publishing House, 2012), 112–13, ¶161J.

3. Same-sex practices

We come now to what I have called the "presenting issue"—Adam's call for a middle-way solution on the question of same-sex practices.[21] The chapter is essentially the manuscript of a sermon he preached in his church in 2004. He collected more than one hundred stories from people in his congregation who self-identified as homosexual, once considered themselves homosexual, or had family members who were homosexual. He notes that reading the stories of real people in his congregation led him to "a place of tremendous inner turmoil," and that he would have changed his sermon topic had he not already announced to his congregation what he planned to preach about that Sunday.

Since I will devote the next chapter to this topic, I will only make a few general comments here about the text of Adam's sermon. He clearly functions from experiential data from his congregation over and against Scripture and tradition. After explaining to his congregation what progressives think and why they want to change the UMC position on same-sex practices, and then traditionalists and why they do not, Adam states rather bluntly, "All of this remains simply hypothetical until we consider actual cases of people who are homosexual."[22] He goes

---

21. Hamilton, *Seeing Gray,* 165–87.
22. Ibid., 179.

on to suggest that our ideals about such things are only possible when we don't actually know anyone affected by them. Hearing the stories of people in his congregation, for example, tests our hypotheses and forces us to modify our views.

All of this sounds rather harmless, right? I want to suggest that it is, in fact, quite problematic. All of us understand today that we read the Bible in our own cultural and personal contexts. We also understand that we cannot interpret Scripture and do our theological work in isolation from real-life situations. None of us should want to. But the clear teaching of Scripture, which Adam himself sees as condemning same-sex intimacy,[23] is *not* "simply hypothetical." If we take the Methodist quadrilateral seriously, we use reason, tradition, and experience to confirm and interpret Scripture. Not the other way around.

In one especially revealing moment in his sermon, Adam says, "I know the Bible . . . but when I listen to the stories [of people in the congregation], I find myself torn."[24] He says he is neither liberal nor conservative, and doesn't have the answers to this problem but sees "through a glass dimly," relying on the apostle Paul's famous line in 1 Corinthians 13:12. Paul, of course, is

---

23. Hamilton, *Seeing Gray*, 187n3.
24. Ibid., 184.

comparing love to various spiritual gifts, especially speaking in tongues, prophecy, and knowledge. In the end, Paul offers a superior way—a way characterized by faith, hope, and love, the latter being the greatest of all. Wesley understands these three together as "the sum of perfection on earth," while "love alone is the sum of perfection in heaven."[25] Love is greater than all the spiritual gifts combined because it is "an even better way" (1 Cor. 12:31). And as the apostle explains, love endures forever while prophecies, tongues, and knowledge are ephemeral blessings (13:8).

The very nature of this love is the issue. A pastor's love for the congregation should lead him or her to warn the flock of behavior that is condemned in Scripture. It isn't sufficient to suggest, *I know what the Bible says on this, but when I hear the experiences of the flock of God, I am torn over what to say.*[26] Adam is clearly a gifted pastor

---

25. John Wesley, *Explanatory Notes upon the New Testament,* 4th American ed. (New York: Lane and Scott, 1850), 437.

26. Please remember in this discussion that Adam concedes that "the Bible clearly teaches that God's design for marriage is heterosexuality and that there is something important about the male and female complementing each other, not simply physiologically, but also emotionally and spiritually" (*Seeing Gray,* 186, and see also 187n3). Earlier I critiqued his next sentence: "At the same time, I believe that there are those who do not fit the norm of Scripture." Elsewhere, Adam has nuanced this considerably in an attempt to minimize the force of the "handful of scriptures" on same-sex intimacy; Adam Hamilton, *When Christians Get It Wrong* (Nashville, TN:

with a heart full of love for his people. I love his passion for ministry. One wonders, however, if his flock would be better served by a position that says, *I know that what the Bible says on this issue is hard and confusing, but I urge you to conform to that teaching for the edification of your own soul in ways we cannot now understand* (we'll come to some pastoral specifics in the next chapter).

Adam's approach in this chapter is also an example of G. K. Chesterton's misplaced humility (the "dislocation of humility" we discussed in the previous chapter). His own "tremendous inner turmoil" drives his incredible pastor's heart, resulting in hesitancy about Scripture's teaching on same-sex intimacy. It is admirable to express humbly one's inner turmoil and passion for the flock. But that same humility and hesitancy has been misplaced and located on Scripture, doctrine, or in this case, sexual practices.

Adam concludes his sermon with the commitment that his congregation, the Church of the Resurrection, will not offer all the answers, and will admit they're struggling over this question. They are called simply to love people.

Abingdon Press, 2010), 85–105, and esp. 92 for the "handful of scriptures" quote, although he says something similar frequently in that chapter. Of course, we don't formulate our theology on the basis of the *quantity* of textual references on any given subject. Otherwise the doctrine of the Trinity would still be in doubt. Adam's interpretive method in *When Christians Get It Wrong* is itself worthy of book-length treatment.

"[W]e will be a church that . . . loves nonreligious and nominally religious people, that loves gay and straight people. We will be a church where people who struggle can know that they will be loved." To this conclusion, I can add "Amen." He essentially exemplifies how a local congregation should respond to the question of same-sex intimacy. In this, he is also exemplifying how any of our UMC local churches should live into our Social Principles on human sexuality.

> We affirm that all persons are individuals of sacred worth, created in the image of God. All persons need the ministry of the church in their struggles for human fulfillment, as well as the spiritual and emotional care of a fellowship that enables reconciling relationships with God, with others, and with self. . . . We will seek to live together in Christian community, welcoming, forgiving, and loving one another, as Christ has loved and accepted us. We implore families and churches not to reject or condemn lesbian and gay members and friends. We commit ourselves to be in ministry for and with all persons.[27]

In this way, Adam Hamilton has provided a beautiful example of how to fulfill this commitment in the local church. Of course, the portion of the *Discipline*'s

---

27. *2012 Book of Discipline*, 111, ¶161f.

statement omitted in this quote by ellipsis (. . .) is the famous "incompatibility" clause: "The United Methodist Church does not condone the practice of homosexuality and considers this practice incompatible with Christian teaching." And this statement is matched by a later restriction prohibiting "self-avowed practicing homosexuals" from being "certified as candidates, ordained as ministers, or appointed to serve in The United Methodist Church."[28]

This is the real issue, isn't it? We might say that Adam exemplifies how a local congregation should love people, and minister to those experiencing same-sex attraction. But he doesn't deal with the denomination's debate over ordination in this chapter. The gray area he proposes between extremes is in many ways already stated as an ideal in our *Discipline*, although many churches struggle with how to be as loving and caring as they should. On the topic of ordination, we must admit we're at a fork in the road. On this point, Adam hasn't offered a gray, middle-way solution at all.

4. Warfare

Our walk through the difficult issues next turns to the question of justifiable warfare versus pacifism.[29] Adam

---

28. *2012 Book of Discipline,* 220, ¶304.3.
29. Hamilton, *Seeing Gray,* 189–210.

publishes here a position paper he wrote for his church in March 2003, just as America was entering war with Iraq. He asserts that he is no pacifist, although he was opposed to the war in Iraq. He considers the case the US government was making at the time for going to war with Iraq, and raises serious questions and objections about its case. Along the way he mentions that he supported the Gulf War in 1991 because Iraq had invaded the neighboring country of Kuwait. That was a case of justifiable war, in Adam's opinion. But this time, he concludes there is insufficient cause for going to war with Iraq. His position paper is clear, and amazingly prescient. He delivered the paper to his congregation March 1, 2003. Nineteen days later, the United States invaded Iraq. As we all know, there were no weapons of mass destruction, and the debate about the war will likely continue indefinitely.

Adam's position paper is excellent, and raises the very questions Christians need to ask of our government whenever war is raised as a possible response. Near the end of his paper, he traces the criteria for justifiable warfare that have been part of just-war theory in the church since the early fourth century AD.[30]

---

30. I traced the same criteria in a general presentation of the two positions, pacifism versus justifiable warfare, with similar conclusions. Bill T. Arnold, *1 and 2 Samuel*, NIV Application Commentary (Grand Rapids, MI: Zondervan, 2003), 102–4.

Augustine and Ambrose formulated the first Christian definitions of justifiable warfare. Most of our thinking today still goes back to their formulations, including the criteria Adam presents. Against pacifism, the just-war position affirms that sometimes our respect for human life compels Christians to support the use of force to protect and defend victims from attackers. Motivation is the key. Force cannot be driven by selfish desire but by the desire to intervene to save others. Just-war theorists maintain it is not the work of love to turn the other cheek of another nation so they may be struck a second time. So the various criteria of just cause, last resort, legitimate authority, proportionality, and others are helpful ways of determining when war is justifiable or not.

In hindsight, of course, Adam was exactly right to question the invasion of Iraq. His position paper is especially helpful because our current Social Principles are too vague about any conditions under which war is justifiable, while making a strong statement against warfare in general.[31] And Adam's chapter is an instructive test case as an example of when Christians of like mind about justifiable warfare in general will disagree about specific occasions when war is just or needed. Since he lifts the 1991 Gulf War as an example of justifiable warfare, and by implication in a number of references to Adolf Hitler

---

31. *2012 Book of Discipline,* 140, ¶165C.

the justifiable use of force in World War II, it might have been instructive to use the more complicated case of the thirteen-year war in Afghanistan.

Either way, Adam's position stated so clearly and helpfully here is no compromise or third-way solution between pacifism and just-war theory. Adam articulates the majority view of Christians for sixteen hundred years, since the end of Roman persecution of Christians when the church first began to explore the legitimate use of force. I agree with his general approach. His is no gray-area position. He has effectively taken a position on the side of justifiable warfare.

5. Politics

The final controversial issue in Adam's presentation is the role of faith in today's political scene.[32] This is Adam's attempt to find a way through our current deadlock in American politics. Both the Democrats and Republicans have become more and more entrenched in hardline ideological views, and the two have become increasingly

---

32. Hamilton, *Seeing Gray*, 211–17. There is one more chapter in Adam's book under this category, chapter 22, "A Worthy Vision for America" (*Seeing Gray*, 219–26). Here he encourages Christians to be good citizens of the United States by raising questions about foreign policy and national consumption, as a vision for America and as a means of creating a "better, safer, and more just world." It is not clear to me how this relates to the objective of seeing gray in a world of black and white.

polarized. Adam's discussion raises the question of what Christians should look for in a presidential candidate. Given a choice between candidates of equal skill, preparation, and ability, Adam urges voting for the Christian over the agnostic. But Christian faith is not essential to being a good president. Adam would look for someone identified with neither the religious right nor the religious left but is instead a bridge-builder "between these two competing pictures of Christianity." He recommends looking for presidential candidates who are "capable of seeing gray in a world of black and white."

These are common sense and helpful suggestions from Adam. Many of his suggestions related to ethics, abortion, warfare, and politics are pastoral and balanced. Yet whether or not we might consider these views centrist or middle-way solutions is unclear. On the question of same-sex practices, especially as it relates to the question of whether the UMC should endorse and celebrate same-sex intimacy on par with heterosexual practices, Adam hasn't offered a gray area, middle-way solution at all.

This takes us back to an earlier question. How is it helpful to lump together assorted controversial issues and treat them together simply because they are all controversial? Each debated issue has its own complex set of problems. At times, a gray area, middle-way solution is possible. At other times, we simply must admit we stand at a fork in the road, dividing us into distinct and separate paths. It does not follow that because one or more of these contentious questions has a compromise solution, we can or should try to compromise on all the rest (recall the Fallacy of Ambiguity in chapter 1). Neither does it follow that any such compromise or tertium quid solution is necessarily progress.

The Left-Handed Cyclist

Before coming to the presenting issue in the next chapter, I return briefly to the question of how the debate has been framed in The United Methodist Church as a choice between holiness or hospitality. And here we have a problem. These are not conflicting opposites, between which we must choose. Nor are they mutually exclusive. It's a fundamental category mistake to frame the debate in this way.

Reducing the arguments in this debate to a choice between holiness and hospitality is like asking me: *Are you right-handed, or have you learned to ride a bicycle instead?* My right-handedness is a fact of my identity. My ability to ride a bicycle is an acquired skill, which is a good thing. But it's not related to my right-handedness. If I were left-handed, I could be just as good a cyclist. And whether I am right- or left-handed, I could know how to ride a bicycle. I may know how to ride a bicycle but choose never to do so. But I am still right-handed, regardless of my transportation preferences.

My point is, these two—holiness and hospitality—are not equal virtues. The first, holiness, is a central theme of both Old and New Testaments, a unifying attribute of the essence of God, and the origin and source of all derived holiness for holy places, holy things, holy times and seasons, and holy people.[33] This is central to Christian faith and doctrine.

Hospitality, on the other hand, is a wonderful virtue, focusing as it does on a welcoming and inviting reception for a guest on the part of the host. Furthermore this is a virtue that we should all learn to practice, and comes more naturally for some than for others (like riding a bicycle). Such a virtue is enhanced and intensified by other Christian virtues, even by Christian love itself. At the same time, it must be admitted that hospitality need not be Christian at all. An unbeliever or adherent of another faith can be hospitable. Holiness is a doctrinal essential of Christianity, revealed in Scripture, confirmed by reason, and illumined by tradition. Hospitality isn't.

Rather than thinking in these two categories, it would be more helpful in our current crisis in the UMC

---

33. Allan Coppedge, *Portraits of God: A Biblical Theology of Holiness* (Downers Grove, IL: InterVarsity Press, 2001), 39–53.

to use an entirely different set of categories. Perhaps our debate on same-sex intimacy would be best informed by H. Richard Niebuhr's classic study of Christian inter-action with culture. In one of the most influential books of the twentieth century, he offered a schematization of different ways in which believers through the centuries have interacted with the world.

Niebuhr defines first a sectarian, separatist impulse, "Christ against culture." These are Christians who see the world as hopelessly corrupt. As members of the kingdom of God, they see no alternative but to withdraw from the sinful world. This impulse is evident throughout the history of Christianity in various groups, separatists of all types, including many forms of fundamentalism today. Second, at the opposite end of the spectrum, Niebuhr identifies "the Christ of culture,"[34] Christians who sense no great tension between church and world. These understand Christ through culture, selecting from Christian doctrine and the teachings of Scripture certain points that seem to agree with what is best in human culture. Niebuhr compared these Christians who inter-pret Christ in cultural terms to the Gnosticism of the early years of Christianity. Niebuhr at times refers to these

---

34. H. Richard Niebuhr, *Christ and Culture* (New York: Harper, 1951); and for convenient summary and commentary, see John G. Stackhouse Jr., "In the World, but . . . : Richard Niebuhr's Christ and Culture is 50 years old," *Christianity Today,* April 2002, 80.

first two types as "radical Christianity" and "cultural Christianity."

Between these two extremes are three mediating positions. These are all three labeled "Christ above culture," but with three distinct "families among them." One mediating position is called "Christ above culture" (again), and considers all that is good in human culture a gift from God. This centrist approach believes the good features of human culture need revelation and mediation in order to be fully realized. Next, "Christ and culture in paradox," are Christians who feel a particular tension between church and world, and seek both to hold together and distinguish loyalty to Christ with responsibility for culture. These Christians live in conflict, understanding the corrupt nature of human culture but at the same time recognizing that we cannot be completely removed from it. Finally, Niebuhr identifies "Christ the transformer of culture."[35] These Christians have a somewhat more optimistic view of culture, seeking to transform culture rather than rejecting it, assimilating it, or simply living in tension with it. These last three options share more in common with each other than with either of the first two.

There are certain problems with Niebuhr's definitions, and the categories are not always entirely helpful.

---

35. Niebuhr, *Christ and Culture*, 119.

But for our purposes, it may be helpful to consider the three mediating positions between separatists and accommodationists (that is, between those who withdraw from culture and those who conform to it). And furthermore, the fifth category, "Christ the transformer of culture," captures the spirit of the Wesleyan renewal movement of the eighteenth century, and tracks nicely the mission statement of The United Methodist Church: ". . . to make disciples of Jesus Christ for the transformation of the world."[36] Perhaps exploring Niebuhr's fifth category would be more helpful for framing our debate than forcing United Methodists into a holiness-hospitality straitjacket.

Culture in the United States is changing. There can be no mistake about that. The question we've raised in this chapter is whether it would be progress for the church to change the UMC stance against same-sex practices. To do so would essentially be to fall into the Christ-of-culture trap Niebuhr has described, to accommodate to cultural changes rather than offering the Christian ideals of Scripture to our culture. It would make The United Methodist Church another example of cultural Christianity in Niebuhr's words. To yield this point would also make of culture a fifth element of the Methodist quadrilateral. Regardless of the use of reason,

36. *2012 Book of Discipline,* 91, ¶120.

tradition, and experience to interpret Scripture, culture would become the driving force in the church.

The question, then, is whether the UMC should endorse and celebrate same-sex intimacy. Would this be progress? Would this lead us to a utopian reformation of Christianity? A reformation of The United Methodist Church? Or would such a decision be a detour, taking us farther and farther away from utopia and the kingdom of God?

When our three sons were young, we dreaded the twelve-hour trip to visit their grandparents. No sooner than we were on the road, only an hour or so toward our destination, one of them would usually say, "Are we there yet?" So it is with our journey to utopia. For forty years, the UMC has been waylaid by our debates over human sexuality. Are we close to utopia yet, that ideal kingdom of God we all seek? Not even close.

6

Homosexuality at the Center[1]

T hus far, I have used *Seeing Gray in a World of Black and White* as representative of the approach I want to critique. Such an approach seeks a middle-way compromise on the question of human sexuality. I chose Adam Hamilton's book because it has been so influential in the debate in The United Methodist Church. I have shown that agreement on *some* controversial issues is indeed possible. These moral dilemmas may, in fact, have alternative third-way options that are both possible and preferable, and sometimes even offer progress.

---

1. A chapter title borrowed from Adam Hamilton's book *Seeing Gray in a World of Black and White: Thoughts on Religion, Morality, and Politics* (Nashville, TN: Abingdon Press, 2008), 165–87.

But this is not always so. Sometimes we must admit we stand at a fork in the road, and we simply must choose between two options. In these cases we must admit that no compromise or tertium quid solution is possible, let alone preferable and progressive.

I return now to the presenting issue for The United Methodist Church today. This debate brings the church to a fork in the road. Few of us would deny that the question of same-sex practices is the most important question before us today—the presenting issue. Specifically, the question is whether or not we will someday condone and celebrate same-sex intimacy, including perhaps bisexual, transgendered, pansexual, and polysexual intimacy, as well as blessing same-sex marriages and ordaining gay and lesbian ministers.[2]

I believe the church will eventually modify or revise the incompatibility clause in our Social Principles.[3] But

---

2. How the church might understand monogamous faithful marriages for bisexuals remains an open question; William J. Abraham, "The Church's Teaching on Sexuality: A Defense of The United Methodist Church's *Discipline* on Homosexuality," in *Staying the Course: Supporting the Church's Position on Homosexuality,* ed. Maxie D. Dunnam and H. Newton Maloney (Nashville, TN: Abingdon Press, 2003), 15–31, esp. 19.

3. "The United Methodist Church does not condone the practice of homosexuality and considers this practice incompatible with Christian teaching" (*2012 Book of Discipline,* 111, ¶161F, and see the corresponding prohibition related to the qualifications for ordination at 220, ¶304.3). Attempts have so far failed at General

that is not the heart of the question. We will certainly find new and better ways to express our convictions on human sexuality. The real question is: Should we continue to hold an understanding of Christian teaching on human sexuality as affirmed "only with the covenant of monogamous, heterosexual marriage"[4] or should we instead support and condone same-sex practices as equally blessed and acceptable in Christian teaching? These are the two options before us, between which we must choose.

Our theological resources and doctrinal heritage drive the UMC to choose traditional Christian teaching on human sexuality; that is, sexual relations as restricted to monogamous, heterosexual marriage. Those theological resources include hamartiology, soteriology, and ecclesiology, as we shall see (I will give brief definitions to each and explain their relevance in this chapter). In

---

Conference to replace these with positive statements condoning and blessing monogamous heterosexual marriage as the norm for sexual relations according to Christian teaching. The qualifications for ordination could then be changed as well to state that UMC ministers will either (a) live faithfully in Christian marriage, defined as a sacred union between one man and one woman, or (b) live faithfully in Christian celibacy (Matt. 19:12; 1 Cor. 7:1–16). Anyone unwilling to commit to one of these two options would not be certified as candidates, ordained as ministers, or appointed to serve in the UMC.

4. *2012 Book of Discipline*, 110, ¶161F.

order to explain how and why this is so, I turn now to three myths about same-sex intimacy that impede the contemporary debate. These three myths have also made it nearly impossible for the church to move beyond the debate to fulfill its mission of making disciples of Jesus Christ for the transformation of the world.[5]

Myth #1: It's About Orientation

The use of the term "orientation" has won the argument in American culture. The subtle implication is that one's sexual orientation is like one's directional location in relation to the points of a compass. One person has a north-south orientation. Another has an east-west orientation. And so, it is assumed, heterosexual and homosexual orientations are God-given. Some speak of a bisexual orientation. Many in American culture today take for granted the idea that sexual orientation is inborn

_____

5. Joy J. Moore has used similar language to speak of myths and rationalizations in the arguments of those wishing to move the church away from traditional understandings. I have learned much from her discussion, while taking the myths discussion in a different direction. Joy J. Moore, "Contentious Conversations: Myths in the Homosexuality Debate," in _Staying the Course: Supporting the Church's Position on Homosexuality,_ ed. Maxie D. Dunnam and H. Newton Maloney (Nashville, TN: Abingdon Press, 2003), 115–21; _2012 Book of Discipline,_ 91, ¶120.

and fixed. Others argue it develops gradually during a person's lifetime.[6]

The truth is, we cannot be sure what homosexuality is or why it exists. At the foundation of this myth of orientation, and making it possible, is a theory of *essentialism*, which holds that "homosexual behavior is a manifestation of some inner essence, perhaps biological or psychological, is relatively stable over time, and characteristic of a distinct minority of the population."[7] This theory of essentialism is where our culture gets the idea of homosexual orientation.

This sociological theory of essentialism has fallen on hard times of late. A more likely approach, known as *constructivism*, argues that homosexuality is merely a social label. What we now call homosexuality is really only a behavior interpreted in different ways by different societies throughout history. It is not an inner essence that some people have and others do not. It's not an orientation characteristic of a minority of any population, such as 5 or 10 percent of the population.

---

6. And the terminology has found its way into the church's debate about same-sex practices; *2012 Book of Discipline*, 111, ¶161F.

7. David F. Greenberg, *The Construction of Homosexuality* (Chicago, IL: University of Chicago Press, 1988), 485. For much of what follows on the constructivist view, see his impressive volume, especially the concluding chapter, 482–99.

Basically, what we think of as homosexuality is a social construction invented by Western societies. An exhaustive and comparative sociological study of same-sex behaviors in the ancient Near East and the Greco-Roman world, combined with data from China, Japan, and North and South America, resulted in the conclusion that the concept of a homosexual person was the result of a combination of social forces at work in nineteenth-century Europe.[8] In fact, most sociologists admit that nearly all humans have the *capacity* to be attracted to members of the same sex, without having these feelings labeled or actualized as homosexuality and certainly without realizing a lifelong identity as a homosexual.[9]

The idea of a fixed same-sex orientation should be abandoned in the discussion. The concept of a homosexual inner essence, fixed at birth, won't hold up under close scrutiny.[10] It is no longer possible to argue

---

8. These forces included urbanization, the rise of science (which led people to see their feelings as deterministic), medicine, and bureaucracy; see Greenberg, *Construction of Homosexuality*, 301–454.

9. On the impossibility of arriving at certainty regarding orientation, see Greenberg, *Construction of Homosexuality*, 488–89. And for the incongruence of a bisexual orientation, see 488n13.

10. Such identifications strike me as a modern form of ancient Gnosticism. We are told, your physical body is merely a vessel for the real you (perhaps your soul). The real you is trapped in a body

that same-sex behavior is a static condition or trait, like being black or white, brown-eyed or blue-eyed. And just as it will no longer work to refer to homosexuality as an abstraction, or orientation, so it will no longer work to identify oneself according to one's sexual actions. One day we may learn to stop objectifying our personal identities by body organs and sexual conduct, especially in the church. We have rich theological resources to understand each other as created in the image of God, which means our personal identity is found in our relationship to God and to each other. I am a Christian. Also a son, husband, father, and friend. The fact that I am also a male heterosexual is secondary to my Christian identity, and to identify me in those terms is sadly inadequate and reductionistic. It may be enough for my tax forms or the US Census Bureau. But it's not sufficient in the church.[11]

---

that may or may not have anything to do with who you really are. So, the high school boy who experiences same-sex attraction is told to come out of the closet. To do so is being genuine and authentic, so he may love himself for who he really is. On the nonsense of being true to oneself, see the quote from Harry G. Frankfurt in the next chapter.

11. And as a reminder, it should be noted that the Scripture nowhere uses anything like orientation or essentialism to categorize human beings along the lines of sexual preferences; Richard B. Hays, "The Biblical Witness Concerning Homosexuality," in *Staying the Course: Supporting the Church's Position on Homosexuality,* ed. Maxie D. Dunnam and H. Newton Maloney (Nashville, TN: Abingdon Press, 2003), 65–84, esp. 74.

Myth #2: It's About Liberation

The next myth to expose is the idea that the church's teaching about sex is hurtful, enslaving, old-fashioned, closed-minded, or any number of other undesirable and repressive traits. Based on this myth, the argument for dropping the church's stance against same-sex practices is about liberating people from an authoritarian, even tyrannical past.[12] It's about expanding the sexual liberty afforded heterosexuals since the 1960s. As a natural next step after the sexual revolution, it is now time to offer such liberty of expression to homosexuals, it is argued. The Bible's unreasonable strictures against same-sex intimacy are embedded in societal constraints that are unhealthy and need to be sloughed off so we can get on with improving the lives of people.

This myth is really only a subset of a much larger myth prevalent in our culture today. It runs something like this. The highest values we cherish in Western society are the ideals of individual rights and liberties, a nation's right to self-rule, separation of church and state, and the

---

12. In extreme forms, this view argues for "the fundamentally bisexual nature" of all human beings, and believes a truly liberated society might regard bisexuality as the ideal state. People would fall in love and partner with each other without regard to gender. See Dennis Altman, *Homosexual: Oppression and Liberation* (New York: Outerbridge & Dienstfrey, 1971).

freedom of inquiry through science. All of these values, according to this myth, were made possible through a slow process of secularization. These advances were not possible in Medieval and Renaissance Europe because the church was too influential and people were so thoroughly religious. The grip of Christianity especially was crippling. Only with the birth of science in the sixteenth and seventeenth centuries, when religion was partitioned and limited in its influences, were modern advances made possible. According to this line of thought, oppressive Christianity needed to be overcome and ignored in order for these modern values to evolve, including liberty, freedom, and tolerance. The process of secularization—slow moving but inevitable—saved modern society from the straitjackets of religion.

First let's consider the church's teaching on sex before turning to the larger question of how our values in Western society developed. Just below the surface of our debate on acceptable or unacceptable sexual practices is the sexual revolution of the watershed 1960s. It is no exaggeration to suggest the sexual revolution was as important a turning point as the Communist revolution in terms of its influence on the twentieth century.[13]

---

13. As argued by Mary Eberstadt, *Adam and Eve After the Pill: Paradoxes of the Sexual Revolution* (San Francisco, CA: Ignatius Press, 2012), 24–35.

Regardless of whether you see the sexual revolution as a good or bad thing, we can agree it certainly changed everything. Among other consequences of the revolution, it made recreational sex mainstream for the first time in human history, freeing sex from reproduction (because of contraceptives). It led to young people becoming sexually active much earlier, pushed marriage later in life, and some would argue increased divorce, cohabitation, illegitimacy, and many other unexpected consequences.[14]

To illustrate these dramatic changes in American culture, Mary Eberstadt of the Hoover Institution invites us to imagine two women. Betty is a thirty-year-old housewife in 1958; her granddaughter Jennifer is thirty today.[15] Consider their attitudes toward sex and food. Betty has few strong opinions about food. She has personal preferences, of course, but she understands these as personal. She frankly doesn't spend much time thinking about food as anything but, well . . . food. Betty does, however, have strong opinions about sex. She believes nonmarital sexual activity is harmful to everyone involved, and this is so because of universal

---

14. Including even the suggestion that the modern welfare state is a result of the sexual revolution, harming especially the most powerless of society—children and lower-class women; Eberstadt, *Adam and Eve*, 36–77.

15. Ibid., 98–104.

moral imperatives. It's about rules of standard behavior, a simple matter of right and wrong. She believes everyone would be better off believing as she does, and following these universal moral principles.

Today, Betty's granddaughter, Jennifer, has flipped these two perceptions around. She has her own preferences, of course, when it comes to sex. But they're personal and have nothing whatsoever to do with any universal moral imperatives. As long as sex is between two (or more) consenting adults, Jennifer thinks of sex pretty much as Betty thought of food. She strives to be consistent and genuine in her libertarian conviction about sex, and therefore Jennifer is pro-abortion, pro-gay marriage, etc. Jennifer does, however, have strong opinions about food. She believes in healthy eating, which for her means she is opposed to industrialized breeding, to genetically enhanced fruits and vegetables, and to pesticides or other artificial ingredients. She minimizes her dairy intake, and cooks tofu as much as possible. Jennifer believes a moral case can be made for vegetarianism, and believes others should believe and do as she does when it comes to food.

In fewer than sixty years, "the moral poles of sex and food have been reversed."[16] Betty thinks food is a matter of personal taste, whereas sex is governed by universal

---

16. Eberstadt, *Adam and Eve*, 104.

morals. Jennifer things exactly the reverse. Eberstadt calls this a "transvaluation of values," which is one of many consequences of the sexual revolution leaving devastating consequences in American society today. My point is, we often think that we have evolved beyond the simplistic views of the 1950s, especially related to sex. We deceive ourselves into thinking that this is liberating (Eberstadt's "the will to disbelieve").

The truth is, the sexual revolution of the 1960s destigmatized and demystified nonmarital sex, reducing sex to a kind of "hygienic recreation in which anything goes so long as those involved are consenting adults."[17] This is the world secular liberationist philosophers dreamed about for centuries. And now we have it. In reality, as Eberstadt shows, we have merely transferred our values from sex to other aspects of life, creating an imaginary view of sex without consequences. The results have been devastating for both men and women in our society, and especially for the living conditions of children and for lower-income women. The church's teaching about sex is not the problem, and liberation from that teaching has not provided healthy freedom. On the contrary, it can be argued that the church failed to influence culture in the 1960s, losing its voice and failing to condemn nonmarital sexual practices of all kinds.

---

17. Eberstadt, *Adam and Eve*, 24.

So much for liberty provided by the sexual revolution! The heritage of that revolution has been enslavement and poverty rather than greater freedom. And the 1960s views of human sexuality are related to the gradual secularization of American culture generally. This is only part of a larger myth that assumes the values we cherish in Western society were made possible by a gradual process of secularization. What we so often fail to remember is that modern science emerged in sixteenth-century Europe precisely *because* of the religious contributions of Christianity, not in spite of Christian influence. Science was not born, as is often assumed, when modern scholars finally threw off the blinders of religious ignorance. On the contrary, science was the direct result of theological convictions unique to Judeo-Christian formulations in Europe, explaining why science was born only in Europe.[18] Science owes its origins to Christianity, and is in some ways a delayed benefit of the Reformation.

But there's more. Those values of our Western society we hold so dear, especially liberty, are not the result of secularization but rather the result of deep reflection on Scripture itself, and especially the Old Testament in the

---

18. For more on this, see Bill T. Arnold, *Introduction to the Old Testament* (New York and Cambridge: Cambridge University Press, 2014), 387–88.

wake of the Protestant Reformation.[19] Liberty is not the result of overcoming and ignoring Christianity. Quite the opposite is true. Christianity made possible the highest virtues and values we cherish most about Western society. The church's teaching on human sexuality is a subset of that magnificent Christian heritage. It simply won't do anymore to argue that changing the church's teaching on same-sex intimacy would be liberating.

Myth #3: It's About Civil Rights

One final myth is the constant refrain that compares today's debate with the civil rights movement of the 1960s. The truth is, there are enough differences, and those differences are so profound between the struggle for civil rights and today's debate about human sexuality as to render the comparison irrelevant. Arguments based on this myth carry no force. It might also be suggested that such a comparison does no service to ongoing efforts to ensure and protect the civil rights of non-European citizens, and perhaps even dishonors the memories of the sacrifices of that struggle during the 1960s.

---

19. Eric Nelson, *The Hebrew Republic: Jewish Sources and the Transformation of European Political Thought* (Cambridge: Harvard University Press, 2010).

Rather than listing all the differences between the civil rights movement and our current debate (some of which should be obvious[20]), it is more instructive to explore two ways in which the comparison breaks down. First, the human rights argument uses a misplaced ethic, because it "*redirects* the dialogue from ethics to hospitality."[21] This redirection of ethics to hospitality is a distraction from the topic, and essentially changes the subject (review the Red Herring Fallacy in chapter 1). Such redirection is accomplished by focusing on violence and hatred directed against homosexuals in our culture. By equating vicious antihomosexual behavior with the church's traditional views on human sexuality, it makes it possible to "eclipse the concerns of morality by highlighting human and civil rights." The result is that the "moral argument disappears in a shift to civility, concentrating on the human right to justice and freedom." This misplaced or shifted ethic will no longer work. The church stands firm on the side of protecting

---

20. Starting with the distinction between oppression on the basis of race (as opposed to sexual behavior), then moving to the social location of African Americans during the Civil Rights Movement, and the extent of systemic and institutional racism. This is not to minimize the problem of sex-based hate crimes in our society, or other deplorable maltreatment of people based on sexual self-identification.

21. Emphasis added. For quotes in this paragraph see Joy J. Moore, "Contentious Conversations," 118.

the civil rights of all, knowing as we do that "all persons are individuals of sacred worth, created in the image of God."[22] The church must be allowed to fight for human and civil rights for *all*, while also calling us *all* to the highest standards of sexuality as discerned by Scripture, reason, tradition, and experience.

Second, the human rights argument misappropriates the civil rights movement itself. In order to explain what I mean, I quote extensively from Joy J. Moore, who makes this case better than I am able to do.

> The effort to change [sexual] moral definitions misinterprets the struggle of past human rights movements. Past coalitions sought to restore full humanity to persons of non-European descent (then viewed as less than human) a century after the elimination of the institution of slavery in America. They requested, not to *change* ethical standards, but to *practice* them. For example, the question of interracial marriage was not based on differing values or inconsistent understandings about marriage and sex. The definition of marriage as the uniting of a man and a woman was not changed. Today's arguments related to same-sex union seek to redefine institutions and change moral categories. . . . Revising moral standards changes

---

22. *2012 Book of Discipline,* 111, ¶161F.

the very ethics that call into question judging a person by birth rather than by behavior. Persons of non-European descent have requested they not be assumed incapable of behaving within the moral and cultural standards of society. Advocates for homosexual practice appeal for a change in cultural mores that will accept particular behaviors traditionally deemed immoral. The former seeks to be allowed to behave within existing ethics, the latter seeks identification by practices presently outside of cultural standards. This is a very different request for rights.[23]

Note especially her argument that the civil rights movement called for an *application* of Christian ethics rather than an *alteration* of those ethics. Of the many differences between the civil rights movement and our current debate, this is without doubt the most profound. Civil rights advocates made an impact on society and on our church not by calling us to change Christian moral standards, but rather by calling us *to live into them*. To make them a reality. Some will counter that condoning same-sex practices today likewise calls us to live into a Christian ideal in the same way civil rights advocates did for racial minorities. But this is a misappropriation of

---

23. Emphasis added. Moore, "Contentious Conversations," 118.

the civil rights movement. Though arousing emotional support, such an argument does not stand up to scrutiny.

So, What's It About?

These three myths—orientation, liberation, and civil rights analogies—each have coordinates in our theological enterprise. As long as the debate is marked by these kinds of arguments, we will make little progress as a denomination. Instead we must turn again to our rich Wesleyan heritage to find answers. First, we need to revisit our understanding of *hamartiology*, investigating the origin, nature, extent, and consequences of sin. As we have seen, the Scripture clearly condemns same-sex practices, but there is no condemnation of individuals who engage in such practices.[24] We are certainly wrong to emphasize one sexual behavior identified in Scripture as falling short of God's highest ideal, while refusing to deal with other sexual brokenness. After the great transgression of Genesis 3, all humans have a sinful nature or orientation. We agree in general principle with other Christians that "original sin" is evident in the lives of all humans. But we Wesleyans also emphasize the "original righteousness" of

---

24. Richard M. Davidson, *Flame of Yahweh: Sexuality in the Old Testament* (Peabody, MA: Hendrickson Publishers, 2007), 169–70.

Genesis 1–2. Sin in our lives is destructive and devastating if left unattended. But it is not irreversible.

This leads us secondly to revisit our *soteriology*, investigating ways in which God leads us to forgiveness, healing, and restoration, in order for us to know him and enjoy him forever. Especially related to our debate on human sexuality, we need continued investigation of "subjective soteriology," which considers the work of the Holy Spirit in the application of God's grace in the process of sanctification. Rather than liberation, our debate needs to explore more profoundly the nature of sanctification.

Finally, we need to revisit our understanding of *ecclesiology*, investigating the nature, function, mission, and ministry of the church. The church universal has a long and rich tradition of resolving controversies in ecumenical church councils. The UMC, in particular, is committed to holy conferencing as a way of hearing each other, deciding on a course of action, and moving forward. The church has committed itself, as it should, given our theological understanding of the sacred worth of all God's creatures, to defending the human and civil rights of all. We all agree to that much, while we continue to debate what would be a truly Christian response to the challenge of today's understanding of same-sex intimacy.

After dispelling these three myths, I close this discussion with brief comments on what the debate should entail. Instead of these myths—orientation, liberation, and civil rights analogies—what would happen if we focused on these:

> It's about sin in our lives.
>
> It's about forgiveness and restoration.
>
> It's about sanctification.

I am painfully aware that this reconfiguration of the debate will not be satisfying to many. But these answers flow appropriately and naturally from our theological resources in the Wesleyan heritage.

Which brings us back to the presenting issue for The United Methodist Church today. At the end of Adam Hamilton's chapter on homosexuality, he concludes that there are certain circumstances in which God's ideal for a person cannot be accomplished. In such circumstances, God blesses a lesser ideal, a "circumstantial will," or what Adam calls God's "Plan B."[25] He concludes

---

25. *Seeing Gray*, 186. Adam also concludes that he would love and accept one of his daughters if she "felt she was homosexual," and that he would welcome her if she brought her partner to his church. Of course he would! As any good father would! But the question before the UMC is whether we ought also to ordain Adam's daughter if she self-identifies as a lesbian, bisexual, or transgendered person. And whether we as a church should celebrate her union with her partner as a Christian marriage.

that homosexuality is one of those circumstances that calls for God's Plan B.

In this conclusion, Adam appeals to the classic study by Leslie D. Weatherhead, *The Will of God*.[26] Weatherhead details (a) the intentional will of God, which is God's ideal purpose for humanity, (b) the circumstantial will of God, in which circumstances are complicated by evil and the intentional will of God cannot be accomplished, and (c) the ultimate will of God, or God's final realization of his purposes. It seems unlikely to me that the definition and understanding of circumstantial will relates to Adam's conclusion of homosexuality as Plan B. Weatherhead has in mind those times when evil brought about by other people acting of their own free will have caused circumstances in which God's intentional will is impossible. This is about finding and doing God's will in the midst of tragic circumstances.

But let us grant the idea for the sake of exploring Adam's conclusion. Are there times we bless and encourage people to live into a plan for their lives that we believe is less than God's ideal purpose for them? Are there people for whom God blesses a Plan B for whatever reason (not simply because of the evil of humanity making Plan A impossible)? I can imagine numerous

---

26. Nashville, TN: Abingdon Press, 1944.

circumstances in a Christian's life when previous actions or decisions have made impossible what might have been God's first and best intention for that individual. Most cases are the result of missed opportunities or sinful choices that have made impossible what might otherwise have been a life-choice or calling. Does same-sex intimacy constitute God's Plan B?

The pastoral implications of this question are enormous. Our Scripture and theology teach us that nothing can separate us from the love of God. And of course we need always to emphasize that same-sex feelings or predispositions do not leave people somehow undeserving of God's love and forgiveness, or of human respect and dignity. But it is entirely another thing altogether to celebrate, embrace, and encourage others to accept same-sex intimacy as God's will for them.

C. S. Lewis wrote a letter in 1954 to his friend Sheldon Vanauken that I find helpful on this question. At the time, Vanauken and his wife were counseling Christians who were asking hard questions about same-gender sexual behavior. They asked Lewis for his opinion, and the following quote is his response. Lewis's phraseology on the subject will sound unguarded in certain ways. I ask you, my twenty-first-century reader, to hear his voice and not necessarily the specific words he uses to refer to same-sex intimacy.

I take it for certain that the *physical* satisfaction of homosexual desires is sin. This leaves the homosexual no worse off than any normal person who is, for whatever reason, prevented from marrying. . . . [O]ur speculations on the cause of the abnormality are not what matters and we must be content with ignorance. The disciples were not told *why* (in terms of efficient cause) the man was born blind (John 9:1–3): only the final cause, that the works of God should be made manifest in him. This suggests that in homosexuality, as in every other tribulation, those works can be made manifest: i.e., that every disability conceals a vocation, if only we can find it, which will "turn the necessity to glorious gain." . . . All I have really said is that, like all other tribulations, it must be offered to God and His guidance how to use it must be sought.[27]

Pastorally, we do well to remind people that Scripture nowhere condemns people who experience same-sex *attraction* or propensities. Instead, the question is whether the church should endorse the idea that same-sex behavior may rightly be accepted and celebrated

---

27. C. S. Lewis, *Yours, Jack: Spiritual Direction from C. S. Lewis,* ed. Paul F. Ford (New York: Harper One, 2008), 241–42; for the quote "Turns his necessity to glorious gain," see William Wordsworth, "Character of the Happy Warrior," line 14.

as God's means of sexual expression. Can it simply be an alternative to heterosexuality? All our theological resources agree that God's purpose for human sexuality is the covenant of marriage between one man and one woman. The church's mission includes calling all people to live into this ideal, which is God's Plan A.

The alternative is a life of self-discipline through celibacy. I close this discussion with the explanation of Bishop Timothy W. Whitaker.

> [T]he church knows the power of human sexuality can also be a destructive force of self-indulgence or exploitation. That is why the church traditionally has balanced affirmation with ascesis or self-discipline. Ascesis involves transfiguring eros (sexual love or desire) into agape (divine love), thus providing a means of grace for one to enter more closely into communion with God. The contemporary culture has been so sexualized that many cannot envision a way of life that does not involve the fulfillment of sexual desire. Yet, the church does envision a way of life that involves spiritual fulfillment and intimacy with other human beings without sexual intercourse. In its long spiritual tradition, the historic Christian community has discovered that eros can offer a false fulfillment—an ecstasy of union that is a substitute for the self-transcendence that comes from union

with God. From the church's perspective, ascesis is not an injustice, but a gift of spiritual experience not possible without it. Of course, this applies to all people, not just to the small minority who experience same-sex attraction.[28]

---

28. Timothy W. Whitaker, "The Church and Homosexuality," http://www.flumc2.org/pages/detail/967, accessed August 8, 2013.

7

Conclusions: Where Do We Go from Here?

The world has no need of a church that sees as much gray as it sees. That may be precisely what the world *wants*: the church as mirror, reflecting the values of the world back upon itself and confirming those values. At times in the history of Christianity, that is what the church has provided. But the world has enough gray without us adding to the confusion.

Like a loving parent providing boundaries and structure for children, the church exists to communicate divine revelation to the world. Its calling is not to be a mirror but a window, offering a view of life and reality made possible by God's grace and revelation. The church's mission is to call the world to leave aside its unhealthy configurations, thought processes, and passions, as the first disciples cast off their fishing nets and boats (Matt. 4:18–22). The church invites the world to become followers of the Messiah, to join Christians everywhere in praise, adoration, and love of God. Along the way, the black-and-white truths of divine revelation are taught, explained, embodied in the church, and offered to the world. The church doesn't exist to find more gray, but rather to study and understand more profoundly the black-and-white truths of God's revelation.

Moreover, Christianity itself will not be renewed or reformed for the next generation by seeing more gray. God's people are forgiven and empowered when they humbly approach God with prayers of confession, seeking God's presence, and turning from sinful behaviors (2 Chron. 7:14). What the world needs most today is what it has needed in every generation—a robust and high-performance church. With Adam Hamilton, I agree that the church and the world will be best served by a holistic gospel, combining personal and social holiness, and having a view of Scripture that appreciates both its divine and human features. I also believe, however, this is not something new. Unlike Adam, I believe the holistic gospel we need today is not something to be created in the twenty-first century by Christians who are able to discern gray. I believe it emerged in the late eighteenth century in the Wesleyan revival, whose leaders scrutinized afresh the black-and-white truths of Scripture in the context of ancient church tradition. And I believe the holistic gospel they preached continues to offer the world the best understanding of Christianity's apostolic faith.

Adam Hamilton's proposal to see more gray in a world of black and white is the sincere and passionate work of a loving and talented pastor. I appreciate his ministry and honor his influence in the church and society. What I have written here is intended to encourage Adam and others to think of these questions in another way, as I myself continue to explore what it means for us to be purveyors of "the faith delivered once and for all to God's holy people" (Jude 3), while at the same time discerning together where God is leading us as a church.

I have demonstrated that Adam's approach in *Seeing Gray* began by neglecting the roomy middle already articulated by our Methodist heritage. He complains about the narrow choices available to Christians today. It's either Falwell or Spong, it seems; the extremism of black or white. Then Adam offers a middle way between these two, the way of gray as a means of reforming Christianity. But on close scrutiny, we found that Adam's way of gray is largely available in our Wesleyan distinctives, and is not a reformed new Christianity at all. In showing that the dilemma between Falwell and Spong is false, he has excluded satisfying answers already provided by Wesleyan thought. And these answers were achieved by our Methodist forebears through rigorous theological reasoning and scrutiny of black-and-white doctrinal distinctives.

Next, Adam proceeds by begging several questions (he makes too many unwarranted assumptions). First, he assumes a middle-way compromise is *always possible* on all the controversial issues before us. I countered that at times we must admit we stand at a fork in the road. Besides making the mistake of assuming such middle-way solutions are always possible, Adam also assumes such solutions would be *always preferable*. I countered that sometimes our impulse to agree for the sake of unity is merely compromising one's principles. And finally, in addition to the mistake of assuming middle-way solutions are always possible and preferable, Adam assumes such solutions would be *always progress*. I countered that the church must stand above culture and work to transform culture. Anything less is a detour away from the ideal kingdom of God, making it the opposite of progress.

In thinking through these issues, I have been reminded of my experiences at two General Conferences of the UMC. Our church has elevated niceness, humility, unity, and inclusiveness to the level of first-order virtues. How this plays out in a church, in which we are also committed to Scripture, reason, tradition, and experience, is yet to be determined.

In the meantime, above the cacophony of voices expressing opinions about what the church ought to do regarding same-sex practices, we hear a constant refrain, which has several variations. It typically encourages you, regardless of whatever else you may think about this issue, above all else *know yourself*; be *true to yourself.* This sentiment seems to embody both humility and honesty. A corresponding sentiment is the assumption that to impose one's view on such a personal and complex question as sexual intimacy is both presumptuous and less than honest. Perhaps it's even dishonest. Each person is simply being true to themselves, true to their own identity, and true to their "nature."

It is hard to know how to respond to these underlying sentiments. How can one possibly be opposed to honesty, humility, and sincerity? But in truth, the elevation of these sentiments in The United Methodist Church has brought us perilously close to walking away from anything theological at all. It creates in our church a crisis of theological reasoning. It comes close to asking us as Christians to suspend our convictions about what we believe to be true for the sake of unity. It implies that what we hold dear in our faith is hardly worth talking to each other about.

One of the leading philosophers of our day has exposed the error of this approach. His comments appear in the context of exploring the prevalence of skepticism in our world today, by which he means the way in which many people deny that we can have any reliable access to objective reality. It is common today for people to reject the possibility of knowing how things truly are. Such antirealist assumptions undermine any confidence in our ability to determine what is true and what is false.

> One response to this loss of confidence has been a retreat from the discipline required by dedication to the ideal of *correctness* to a quite different sort of discipline, which is imposed by pursuit of an alternative ideal of *sincerity*. Rather than seeking primarily to arrive at accurate representations of a common world, the individual turns toward trying to provide honest representations of himself. Convinced that reality has no inherent nature, which he might hope to identify as the truth about things, he devotes himself to being true to his own nature. It is as though he decides that since it makes no sense to try to be true to the facts, he must therefore try instead to be true to himself. But it is preposterous to imagine that we ourselves are determinate, and hence susceptible both to correct and to incorrect descriptions, while supposing that the ascription of determinacy to anything else has been exposed as a mistake. As conscious beings, we exist only in response to other things, and we cannot know

ourselves at all without knowing them. Moreover, there is nothing in theory, and certainly nothing in experience, to support the extraordinary judgment that it is the truth about himself that is the easiest for a person to know. Facts about ourselves are not peculiarly solid and resistant to skeptical dissolution. Our natures are, indeed, elusively insubstantial—notoriously less stable and less inherent than the natures of other things. And insofar as this is the case, sincerity itself is [nonsense]."[1]

The question he raises for Christians, of course, is this idea of *determinacy*. The temptation is to see in his description of skepticism and sincerity in our culture a parallel development in The United Methodist Church. We appear to have abandoned the idea of discerning determinate truth in our theological enterprise, and have turned instead to an attempt to "know ourselves." But, we take pride in "knowing ourselves" sincerely and honestly. We have made ourselves determinate, The United Methodist Church. But as the philosopher notes, this is nonsense. Determinacy must be located outside of and beyond ourselves. And we have rich theological

---

1. Harry G. Frankfurt, *On Bullshit* (Princeton, NJ: Princeton University Press, 2005), 64–67 (emphasis his).

resources locating reality in Scripture, interpreted with the aid of reason, tradition, and experience.

Until the church returns to these theological resources, we will continue to struggle as we make of ourselves the determinate norm for our culture. Thus the problem with the church today isn't that there is too much black and white, but *not enough*. What we really need is less gray, not more.

QUESTIONS
FOR THE READER

CHAPTER 1

1. How should we decide if an issue is black and white, or if it has some ambiguity?

2. Name some other issues in the church that you think have no third way, that are black and white. Do you and your conversation partners agree about these being black-and-white issues? Why or why not?

3. The author points out that Adam Hamilton assumes the quest for the truth creates division and conflict. But is the quest for a third way itself an attempt to get at truth? And what would happen if we decide that truth either doesn't exist—or if it does exist, that it doesn't matter? If we conclude the quest for truth is wrong for the church, would we then argue that such a conclusion is true? Is

it consistent to maintain that such a conclusion is a true statement, and not a false one?

4. The author takes issue with Adam Hamilton's pragmatic approach. If we were to be pragmatic (responsive to what the culture wants) what other things in the church would likely change as well?

5. Are the third ways we look for only relevant for America? What about our relationship with global Methodism? How much influence should global Methodism have on the question of deciding what is black and white? Or what has a third option? How would global Methodism react if third-way policies were to become the rule of the denomination?

CHAPTER 2

1. The author notices that there are many more options than just two. How do we determine which sides get a seat at the table to discuss some sort of compromise?

2. If there truly are extremes, what would the compromise look like? Is there a compromise between good and evil?

3. How do you approach making decisions as a Christian on controversial issues?

4. Name some issues where there does not seem to be a third way.

5. Can you think of some examples where Jesus made a black-and-white statement, leaving no room for gray? What might such examples tell us about looking for third options?

CHAPTER 3

1. Can you think of some examples where Jesus left things open-ended among a number of options? What are some issues where we have Christian liberty to think and let think?

2. What issues have you been countercultural about? Have there been instances where following the clear teachings of Scripture have put you at odds with people who think "it's no big deal"?

3. Does the silence of Jesus on a given issue determine what we should think about that issue? What does the silence of Jesus mean in these debates? How does the author suggest we reason about such an issue?

4. Apply the Methodist Quadrilateral to the issue of same-sex practices. What should The United Methodist Church's position be, given what we say about our process of theological reasoning?

CHAPTER 4

1. The author reasserts the Wesleyan—and Christian— principle that Scripture is normative for our lives.

How does that add to your understanding of a faithful response to the issue of same-sex practices?

2. Discuss the author's "thought experiment" of a conversation between Old Testament prophets and New Testament apostles and writers. How does this experiment put the Methodist Quadrilateral to work. Is this argument persuasive? Why or why not?

3. The author has shown that the Scriptures are clearly against same-sex practices. And he has asserted that Adam Hamilton's third-way solutions on some of the controversial issues are nonexistent, unnecessary, or not preferable. So what are we really arguing about? What are the deeper issues at stake in the debate over same-sex practices?

4. Is the issue of same-sex practices one on which we can think and let think? Why or why not?

CHAPTER 5

1. How many times will we have to look for a third way? As soon as a third way is articulated, there may be serious opposition to it. And then a new third-way would be called for. Do you think third-way solutions could ultimately lead to a meaningless Christianity that is ignored by the culture and valueless as a force in making disciples of Jesus Christ for the transformation of the world?

2. The author points out that on the issues of ethics and abortion, Adam Hamilton's "third way" is already what the UMC says about those controversial issues. If so, there is in reality no unembraced third way to search for at all. But when it comes to same-sex practices, Hamilton essentially ignores how the UMC already possesses and has repeatedly articulated a redemptive theology—with Scripture in the final position of authority. How can a solution be a viable third-way option if it, at the same time, rejects or neglects the core of our beliefs as a denomination?

3. Reflect on the need for pastors to balance their compassion for their flock and sympathy with individuals struggling with same-sex attractions with their responsibility to hold members of their congregation to the highest ideals of Christian ethics.

4. In the last few paragraphs of the chapter, the author warns us about allowing our culture to determine the direction of the church. Discuss some times when the church has accommodated the culture, and what the price was. What about times when the church has defied the culture?

CHAPTER 6

1. The basic arguments of the debate have changed over the past twenty years. What relevance should the culture's changing views of sexuality have on the

church's articulation and proclamation of Christian ethics?

2. If we accept the sexual liberation premise, what is the end point? Are there any sexual practices that are out of bounds? Which sexual practices are "incompatible with Christian teaching," and how would you know?

3. The author suggests that the proper rubric for the church is to see the issue of same-sex practices in terms of "sin, salvation, and the nature and ministry of the church." How should Methodism's teachings on the transformative work of the Holy Spirit guide our thinking on this issue? How should our theology help the church know how to respond to people demanding that the church fully embrace and normalize same-sex practices? What does sanctifying grace look like in such a solution?

CHAPTER 7

1. Of the many critiques that the author offers to Adam Hamilton's proposals, which has been the most persuasive? Why?

2. Have the author's arguments changed your position—or adjusted it—on the controversial issue of the UMC's response to same-sex practices?